Nemesis

Five Years of Tory Rule

A Lesson and a Warning

Nemesis

Five Years of Tory Rule
A Lesson and a Warning

ISBN/EAN: 9783744662215

Printed in Europe, USA, Canada, Australia, Japan

Cover: Foto ©ninafisch / pixelio.de

More available books at **www.hansebooks.com**

FIVE YEARS OF TORY RULE:

A LESSON AND A WARNING.

By "NEMESIS."

"Who may be the Ministers of the Queen is an accident of history; what will remain on that enduring page is the policy pursued and its consequences on her realm. That will much depend upon the decision and determination of the constituencies of the United Kingdom in the impending General Election."—Mr. DISRAELI, *Address to the Electors of Buckinghamshire*, May 20th, 1865.

London:
HODDER AND STOUGHTON
27, PATERNOSTER ROW.
—
1879.

[*All rights reserved.*]

"It is Nemesis that . . . . . seals with the stigma of Parliamentary reprobation the catastrophe of a sinister career."—MR. DISRAELI *on Sir Robert Peel*, June 15th, 1846.

Hazell, Watson, and Viney, Printers, London and Aylesbury.

TO THE

ELECTORS

OF THE

UNITED KINGDOM,

UPON WHOM DEPENDS

THE FUTURE OF THEIR COUNTRY,

THIS

STATEMENT OF FACTS

IS DEDICATED,

IN VIEW OF

THE IMMEDIATE APPROACH

OF

A GENERAL ELECTION.

"The impending General Election is one of no mean importance for the future character of this kingdom."—Mr. DISRAELI, *Address to the Electors of Buckinghamshire*, January, 1874.

PREFACE.

THE design of the following pages is to set before the electors of this kingdom a ready means for judging the character of the existing Government. Its aim is not so much to present arguments as to exhibit facts; in so doing it has to review the Ministerial actions of the past five years, and an endeavour is made to show that, tried by truth, the Administration of which Lord Beaconsfield is the head, has been weighed in the balances and found wanting.

As a statement of facts, the pamphlet partakes more of the nature of a compilation than an essay, and the thanks of the writer are due to the editors of the *Annual Register* and *Hansard's* "*Debates*" for much information and many hints. Should any reader discover an inaccuracy, or fail to perceive some point he may think necessary to the completeness of the work, his communication, addressed under cover to the publisher, will be gladly received.

The value of the frequent quotations from

Lord Beaconsfield's speeches and works may be gathered from an observation of the present Foreign Secretary (then Lord Cranborne) in a debate on the Irish Church in March, 1868: "I am bound to say that the right hon. gentleman will have language of his own which he can quote in support of whatever policy he may feel disposed to adopt; for it is part of the skill of the right hon. gentleman to be able to refer to phrases of his own in favour of any course he may deem it advisable to take." Previous to 1874, the present Premier had done so little and talked so much, that it is only from his oratorical efforts that his policy can be guessed.

The writer would only further express the hope that the information he has been enabled to condense may afford some help to those who, comparing 1874 with 1879, cannot avoid inquiring whether this Government did not find the nation tranquil, prosperous, and honoured, and whether it will not leave it harassed, distressed, and in danger of disgrace.

"NEMESIS."

LONDON, *June*, 1879.

CONTENTS.

	PAGE

I.—THE DEMAND FOR DISSOLUTION 1

II.—1874 AND 1879.—THE PROMISE AND THE PERFORMANCE: SEEKING REST AND FINDING NONE. *The Conservatives in Opposition and in Office.* THE HARASSED INTERESTS. *The Farmers, the Priests, the Publicans, and the Civil Servants* 3

III.—THE TORY POLICY AND THE PUBLIC PURSE: WARS THREATENED; *Russia, Burmah, and Egypt.* WARS COMMENCED; *Afghan and Zulu.* ACCUMULATED EXPENDITURE AND INCREASED TAXATION. *Sir Stafford Northcote's Six Budgets.* TORY AND LIBERAL FINANCE. DEFICIT AND DISTRESS 25

IV.—FAILURES, FIASCOES, AND FABLES:

LEGISLATIVE FAILURES. *Abortive Projects:* the Judicature Bill of 1874, the Scotch Patronage Act, the Public Worship Regulation Act, the Savings Banks Bill, the Pollution of Rivers Act, the Burials Bill, the Colorado Beetle Act, the County Boards Bill, and the Scotch Under-Secretary Bill. *Permissive Bills:* the Artizans' Dwellings Act, the Agricultural Holdings Act, and the Friendly Societies Act. *Reactionary Measures:* the Endowed Schools Act, the Licensing Amendment Act, the Regimental Exchanges Act, the Education Amendment Act, the Royal Titles Act, and the Contagious Diseases (Animals) Act. *"Startling" Successes:* the Merchant Shipping Act, the Factory Act, the Employers and Workmen Act, the Winter Assize Act, the Commons Act, the Prisons Act, and the Irish Intermediate Education Act . . . 57-78

ADMINISTRATIVE FIASCOES. *Proposals Withdrawn:* the Slave Circulars, the Rhodope Grant, the Irish University Scheme, and the Indian Ten Millions Loan. *Jobs Accomplished:* the Slade, Hampton, Fitzgerald, Pigott, and Wellesley appointments; Sir James Elphinstone and Mr. Cavendish Bentinck; the Pimlico reductions; the *Vanguard* and *Mistletoe* disasters; the release of Theodorodi and the appeal for Galley; the muzzled Press. *Duties Evaded:* the cases of Sir Daniel Lange, Chefket Pasha, and Mr. Ogle; the position of Greece. *The Uncalled-for Undertaken:* the purchase of the Suez Canal Shares; the Anglo-Turkish Convention and the acquisition of Cyprus. *Treasury Bench Vacillation:* Lord Cairns and the "Caucus;" Mr. Ward Hunt and the "Paper Fleet;" Mr. Sclater-Booth and County Boards; Mr. Stanhope and Sir Stafford Northcote on the Stock Exchange Commission; Mr. Disraeli and the Printers; Sir M. Hicks-Beach and Irish Sunday Closing; the Ministry and the Colonial Marriages and Education Act Amendment Bills; the Abolition of Municipal Qualifications and the Poor Law Act Amendment Bills; the Lord Advocate and the Law of Hypothec; Mr. Lowther and Sir Stafford Northcote on the Irish Land Act Committee 79-113

MINISTERIAL FABLES. *Contradictions:* Mr. Disraeli and the abolition of the Income Tax, Irish Coercive Legislation, and the Bulgarian Atrocities; The Duke of Richmond on the Government Burials Bill; Sir Stafford Northcote on Lord Beaconsfield's Pigott appointment; Lords Beaconsfield and

Salisbury's Berlin appointments and the "scientific frontier;" Lord Beaconsfield and Colonel Stanley on the Queen's letter to Lord Chelmsford; Sir Stafford Northcote on Lord Beaconsfield's "figure of speech." *Equivocations:* Mr. Disraeli and the Endowed Schools and Royal Titles Bills; Lords Salisbury and Beaconsfield on Batoum; Lord Beaconsfield and Lord Carnarvon; Lord Salisbury and "Titus Oates;" Viscount Cranbrook and "Paragraph IX.;" Lord Beaconsfield and the publication of official papers. *Mis-statements:* Lord Salisbury's "blustering majority;" Lord Salisbury and the Afghan policy; Lords Beaconsfield and Salisbury on the Cabinet dissensions; Lord Beaconsfield and Lord Granville; Sir Stafford Northcote and the Indian troops; Lord Salisbury, the Duke of Richmond, and Marvin; Lord Beaconsfield and Batoum; the Premier and Mr. Gladstone; Mr. Bourke, Mr. Cross, and Theodorodi; Lord Salisbury and the Government censure on Sir Bartle Frere 113-133

V.—PERSONAL GOVERNMENT AND IMPERIALISM . 133

VI.—THE OPPOSITION AND THE DICTATORSHIP . 137

VII.—THE CHOICE OF POLICIES 143

"What is the Tory party unless it represents national feeling? If it does not represent national feeling, Toryism is nothing."—MR. DISRAELI, *Speech at the Lord Mayor's Banquet*, August 13th, 1867.

FIVE YEARS OF TORY RULE.

I.—THE DEMAND FOR DISSOLUTION.

"Dissolve, if you please, the Parliament you have betrayed, and appeal to the people, who, I believe, mistrust you. For me there remains this at least—the opportunity of expressing thus publicly my belief that a Conservative Government is an organised hypocrisy."—MR. DISRAELI *on Sir Robert Peel's Government*, March 17th, 1845.

IF the signs of the times count for anything, a Dissolution cannot be long delayed. The present is the Sixth Session of the Parliament; and though its moribund existence can be strained to a seventh, an eighth is beyond the power even of an Imperialist Premier. As bye-election succeeds bye-election, and the Liberal strength becomes more apparent, the hopes increase of those who believe that a new Parliament will meet a new Ministry. The abandonment by the Conservatives of what ought to have been a good chance in East Cumberland, and the narrow majority by which they won such an apparently safe seat as Canterbury, are the shadows of coming events; and the temptation to prolong a doomed life to its utmost limits must be great. But those who note Ministerial procedure are led to believe, despite the assurances of Conservative Whips and party camp-followers, that there is the possibility of dissolution in 1879, and that any morning they may open their newspapers to find the address of Sir Stafford Northcote to his Devonshire constituents as the signal for the letting out of the waters of political strife. Supply is being pushed through with ominous rapidity, and the accidental success of a moment is waited for to snatch from a surprised country a favourable verdict. It is not of a speedy Dissolution that the critics of Ministerial policy will have to complain; it is against a sudden Dissolution that they will have to guard. Time is on their side; with every month the popular discontent with the present system broadens and deepens; and the longer the Government delay the day of reckoning, the more crushing will be their defeat. For having entered upon a legacy of peace, and having squandered their possession, they draw bills upon the future for their successors to meet. Inheritors of peace and plenty, they will leave disaster and distress; heirs to a six millions surplus, they will bequeath a six millions deficit.

II.—1874 AND 1879.—THE PROMISE AND THE PERFORMANCE.

"He had never employed his influence for factious purposes, and had never been stimulated in his exertions by a disordered desire of obtaining office; above all, he had never carried himself to the opposite benches by making propositions by which he was not ready to abide."—MR. DISRAELI *on Sir Robert Peel*, May 27th, 1841.

"There is no doubt a difference in the right hon. gentleman's demeanour as Leader of the Opposition and as Minister of the Crown. But that's the old story: you must not contrast too strongly the hours of courtship with the years of possession."—MR. DISRAELI *on Sir Robert Peel*, March 17th, 1845.

The claim of any Government upon a renewal of confidence is the fulfilment of its promises. Political pledges, as asserted by statesmen, should be solemnly given and sacredly kept. And if it be found that the more deliberate the promise the more doubtful the fulfilment, those who have practised the art of deceit will deserve, and will receive, a speedy dismissal.

SEEKING REST AND FINDING NONE.

"For nearly five years the present Ministers have harassed every trade, worried every profession, and assailed or menaced every class, institution, and species of property in the country.

Occasionally they have varied this state of civil warfare by perpetrating some job which outraged public opinion, or by stumbling into mistakes which have been always discreditable, and sometimes ruinous. All this they call a policy, and seem quite proud of it; but the country has, I think, made up its mind to close this career of plundering and blundering."—MR. DISRAELI, *letter to "My dear Grey,"* October, 1873.

Five years ago a Dissolution secured the return to the House of Commons of a majority pledged to restore rest to a harassed country. The previous Parliament had done so much that the nation was wearied of work, and desired relaxation rather than reform. Peace was promised, tranquillity assured; the people were to sit in calm contemplation of the past, with no thought for the present, and no fear for the future. But as year by year has rolled away, calm contemplation has given place to acute apprehension; the present is troublous, the future fearful. And the majority of 1874, pledged to peace and quiet, exists in 1879, though it has filled the air with wars and rumours of wars, and has strained the Constitution with a more desperate hand than any Parliament of the past half-century.

It is incumbent upon those who have suffered from these results of Tory rule, to inquire into the reasons of their being so troubled, and to ask whether there shall be no retribution for the past, no relief for the future. To argue that what has been done cannot be undone, that the disgrace inflicted upon the nation is only a further reason for pursuing the same course, and that it is only statesmanlike to look to the future, is to ask for memory to be destroyed, and history to be blotted out. From the experience of the past should be gathered the policy of the present; and the fact that the Government has reduced failure to a system, and filled the cup of disaster to overflowing, is sufficient justification for relegating its members to that shade of Opposition in which, though their criticism may assist, their action cannot destroy.

THE HARASSED INTERESTS.

"Conservatism assumes in theory that everything established should be maintained; but adopts in practice that everything that is established is indefensible. To reconcile this theory and this practice, they produce what is called 'the best bargain'; some arrangement which has no principle and no purpose, except to obtain a temporary lull of agitation."—MR. DISRAELI *in* "*Coningsby.*"

"Here, again, we have the same phenomenon—an opinion steadily maintained by the Conservative when out of office, is changed when in office for the same plea for delay, and the same admission that considerable modification is required. . . . I do not pretend to predict the probable course of the right hon. gentleman at the head of the Government [Mr. Disraeli]. I should as soon undertake to tell you which way the weathercock would point to-morrow."—Viscount Cranborne (*now the* Marquis of Salisbury), *Debate on Mr. Gladstone's Irish Church Resolutions*, March 30th, 1868.

The Government were placed in power principally by the efforts of the publicans, the priests, and the farmers, all of whom hoped, from past protestations and present professions, to have ameliorated some of what they considered their grievances. The publicans wanted the Licensing Act repealed, or, at least, more extended facilities afforded them for the sale of liquor; the priests required the Education Act to be so modified as to put a premium upon denominational education, and to stultify the action of the School Boards; the farmers wished for local self-government, security of tenure, and the repeal of the Malt Tax. With these ends in view, they worked with a will to return a Tory majority. Has that Tory majority fulfilled their expectations? Can publican, priest, or farmer reply in the affirmative?

The Farmers.

"All the country gentlemen knew of Conservatism was that it would not repeal the malt tax, and had made them repeal their pledges."—Mr. Disraeli *in* "*Coningsby.*"

Of all the interests whose injuries required alleviating at the hands of this Government, the agricultural, by tradition, had the strongest claim. Staunch supporters of the powers that be, the farmers have been true to Toryism even when Toryism has proved most false to them. Conservatives have given pledges in abundance of what they would do for this class when in power, but the sops thrown to Cerberus have been but small. And it is not always that a Tory Government has treated the farmers even with these. Under Mr. Disraeli, as Chancellor of the Exchequer, they lost the privilege of keeping sheep-dogs free from tax, and in the debate upon the Budget of 1868, the next year, this was complained of as a hardship and even an impropriety by several members favouring the agricultural interest. To this Mr. Ward Hunt, who, in the meantime, had succeeded to the Chancellorship, replied: "I admit that it is hard upon the shepherd to have to pay five shillings for his dog; but I do not admit that it is hard for the shepherd's employer to have to do so." What "the shepherd's employer" might think of this does not seem to have occurred to the speaker.

The farmers might fairly have expected that with the immense surplus Mr. Gladstone had left with their professed friends, not only would this small but vexatious impost have been removed, but that their old enemy, the Malt Tax, would have been abolished. They had some reason to ask this from the Prime Minister, who had never concealed his opinion * that the tax was a bad one, which ought to be taken off when there was a good surplus. Accordingly in April, 1874, Mr. Joshua Fielden moved that "in the opinion of this House, the Malt Tax ought to be repealed." Cold water was thrown upon the proposition by Sir Stafford Northcote, who, thinking the question "a pretty considerable one," expressed a hope that Mr. Fielden would not go to a division "at so unfavourable a time for his proposition," the unfavourable time being the first occasion on which the "friends of the farmer" had held the seals and a surplus for many years. Mr. Fielden, however, rejected the advice of the Chancellor of the Exchequer, and was overwhelmingly defeated.

This instance of the anxiety of the Conservative Government to benefit the farmer was followed by the production of a measure which was admirably calculated to keep the word of promise to the ear and break it to the hope.

---

* *e.g.*, in debates on Col. (now Sir W. B.) Barttelot's motions on the Malt Tax, April, 1864, and May, 1867, and in the autumn of 1866, in answer to a deputation.

It was in March, 1875, that the Duke of Richmond and Gordon brought before the House of Lords his Agricultural Holdings Bill, which neutralised itself by Section 46 (declaring that nothing in it should prevent landlords and tenants making such agreements as they might think fit, or should interfere with such agreements). In the House of Commons resolute endeavours were made by those who pointed out that liberty of contract needed no new legal sanction, to make the provisions of the Bill directly or indirectly compulsory, but the land-holding influence was too strong, and, as a consequence, the measure very speedily became of none effect. On March 25th of the present year, Mr. B. Samuelson moved for a Select Committee to inquire into the working of the Act and the condition of agricultural tenancies, contending that for its avowed purpose of securing to the tenants compensation for unexhausted improvements it had proved a dead letter. This assertion being met with cries of "No" from the Conservative benches, he proceeded to prove it by reading returns which he had procured from all the counties of England, the net result of which was that in nearly every one its direct effects had been *nil*, and its indirect effects very small.

The motion was supported by Mr. C. S. Read, who observed that the good landlords, for whom the Act was not required, had accepted it; but the needy or grasping ones had, as a rule, rejected it; adding that in the ranks of those who had contracted themselves out of the Act was the Duchy of Lancaster, a Government department. Viscount Sandon and the Chancellor of the Exchequer, however, opposed the motion as entirely unnecessary, and it was rejected by a majority of 166 to 115—51.

Thus on two important questions the farmers' grievances have been discountenanced by the farmers' friends, and in yet another instance a promise to remedy them has proved illusory. In March, 1877, Mr. Clare Read moved a resolution in favour of representative county boards. The Government had issued a whip to oppose the motion, but circumstances were too strong, and Mr. Sclater-Booth, to the astonishment of the House, expressed his feeling that he should be doing an ungracious act if he asked Mr. Read to withdraw it. Sir Walter Barttelot thereupon stated that Mr. Booth, whom he considered his bosom friend on this question, had led him to believe only that morning that "a very different course would be pursued by the

Government;" and he expressed his opinion not only that he had been brought down to the House "under false pretences," but that his "bosom friend" was "neither able nor wishful to carry out the resolution." And events have proved that Sir Walter was not far wrong in his surmise. In obedience to his promise, however, Mr. Booth introduced his first County Administration Bill in January, 1878, declaring that the new county authority would rectify grievances, discharge certain new duties, and guide and direct county policy. But though the Bill was an instalment in the right direction, the Government seem to have had no very strong wish to push it through, and it became one of the "massacred innocents" at the end of the session. Owing to it not being reintroduced at the beginning of this year, Mr. Read threatened to obstruct the progress of the Valuation Bill, and, as a consequence, Mr. Booth brought in his second Bill, which would make it the main business of the new boards to levy the county rate in order to pay the cost of magisterial decisions, and thus bear the odium of an expenditure over which they had no control. The first reception of the measure was decidedly unfavourable, and the Bill has not improved upon acquaintance. Chambers of Agriculture, including the Central, have vented their disapprobation upon it, and Mr. Read has gone so far as to say that the more he looked at it the less he liked it, as it would unsettle everything, settle nothing, and disappoint all sections of the community. After such a declaration from one best competent to judge, the Government will indeed be hardy if they again bring the Bill before the House.

Thus on three main questions have the Ministry deceived their agricultural supporters. Against these the relief given in local taxation and the sop of last year's Cattle Bill (which would ultimately benefit the landlord even more than the tenant) count as little. Such treatment of the farmers has deserved the more attention seeing that it is upon the English counties that the Ministry depend for their existence. But the rural voters will be of a most forgiving turn of mind if they continue to show confidence in those who, with every chance to befriend, have done little but betray.

The Priests.

"'I am all for a religious cry,' said Taper. 'It means nothing, and, if successful, does not interfere with business when we are in.'"—MR. DISRAELI *in* "*Coningsby.*"

The alliance of the Church with the Conservatives, strikingly shown at the last election, was far from a new thing, as for centuries the exclusive sect and the exclusive party had been wedded by the common tie of interest. Deceived as the clergy had occasionally been by their especial friends, they were ready again to trust; and 1874 found them, with scarcely an exception, under the Tory banner. They were soon repaid for their devotion.

In April, 1874, the Archbishop of Canterbury introduced to the Peers the Public Worship Regulation Bill, which was, once and for all, to destroy the growth of Ritualism, and which, though much criticised and considerably altered, passed its crucial stages in the Upper House without a division. In the Commons the late Mr. Russell Gurney was its promoter; and it seemed likely that it would ruffle the tranquillity of this portion of the legislature as little as it had that of its fellow, when Mr. Gladstone's criticisms drew Mr. Disraeli into the field. In the course of one of his speeches on the measure the Premier said: "I take the primary object of this Bill, whose powers, if it be enacted, will be applied and extended impartially to all subjects of Her Majesty, to be this,—to put down Ritualism." And, as if to make this more emphatic, Mr. Disraeli, in another speech, inquired, "What is this Bill, and what does it ask?" And to himself replied: "I have endeavoured before to describe it as a Bill to put down Ritualism, and some have excepted to that description. I am here to repeat it, because I believe it is a true and accurate description of its purpose." The second reading was carried in the Commons, as in the Lords, without a division, and large majorities supported its principal clauses in committee, though some important amendments were inserted. But the haste with which the Bill was run through the House has met with its punishment. The Act is simply unworkable. However flagrant the case with which it has to deal, it only annoys and never ameliorates. More than this, by raising the cry of "persecution," it has had greater effect in creating sympathy for Ritualism than any other enactment of the present generation. So far from Ritualism being "put down," it is stronger than ever; and as soon as some fresh condemnation is gained, so soon is some fresh flaw discovered in the Act.

Having provided a measure with which to worry the clergy, the Ministry sought to balance matters by introducing, in the same session, an

Endowed Schools Bill, which would change the presumption of the law to the detriment of the Nonconformists. To rally the spirits of the supporters of the Establishment, Lord Sandon, who was responsible for the Bill, made a slashing attack upon the Dissenters, with the only effect of rousing them from the lethargy into which they had fallen after the Liberal defeat at the Dissolution. And this rousing had a stranger issue than Lord Sandon could have dreamt, for it caused the sacrifice of the most vital portions of the measure. The Scotch Church Patronage Act, of the same year, failed to make up for these mistakes of policy. As was prophesied at the time, instead of bringing back the Free Kirk to its allegiance, it has raised a cry in Scotland for Disestablishment, which is rapidly becoming irresistible; and none know better than English clergymen of the manner in which such measures react upon the Establishments that remain.

The errors of 1874, which did so much to weaken the clerical forces, were not atoned for by Lord Sandon's Education Bill of 1876, strenuous as were the efforts to turn it strongly to the disadvantage of the Nonconformists; and the Government Burials Bill of 1877, without benefitting the Church by removing a Dissenters' grievance whose continuance weakens it, only served to draw from the House of Lords a declaration that the policy of the vast majority of the clergy was utterly untenable. The conduct of the Ministry on the Colonial Marriages Bill has hastened the day for passing the bishop-hated Deceased Wife's Sister Bill, which can now be only narrowly defeated, even in the House of Lords; and it cannot be said that the measures increasing the Episcopate have done much to make up for all this. The Government, though possessed of a large majority in both Houses, have not ventured to propose that the new bishops shall enter Parliament, thus disconnecting episcopacy and the peerage in a manner which may form an awkward precedent for the Church. It is true that in the present session the Ministry has endeavoured to show repentance for this treatment of the clergy by granting them what is practically a subsidy out of the rates, but there is some probability that the Opposition will have the satisfaction of assisting to relegate such an obnoxious proposal to the limbo where repose various other schemes from the same source. The 85th clause of the Valuation Bill provides that in future the parochial clergy shall not be rated on so much of the tithe as may be required for paying the salary of the necessary curate or curates; and, according to a clerical correspondent of the *Guardian*, this would practically put £150,000 into the pockets of the parsons, a sum which, if capitalised, he reckons to exceed four millions sterling. But Boards of Guardians and Chambers of Agriculture are on the alert against this new scheme of establishmentarian endowment, and opposition is threatened from both sides of the House. Thus, the only project likely to be of much benefit to the clergy will most probably fail; and as for the others that have been named, which have worried and weakened the Church without advantage to the State, their effect will be to swell the Liberal reaction, and to assist in the downfall of the party which professes such ardent love for the Establishment.

The Publicans.

According to the late Mr. J. M. Cobbett, M.P. for Oldham (in a debate in the House of Commons in April, 1864), Mr. Disraeli once distinctly avowed that beer was a necessary of life. Perhaps it was because of this belief, mingled with the sentiment that he is " on the side of the angels,' that the Prime Minister so readily consented to that alliance of "Beer and Bible" which did so much for him five years since. However that may be, the fact remains that the licensed victuallers did for once look upon the Conservatives as their special friends, and it was not three months after the General Election before their services to the cause were attempted to be paid for by the introduction of a Bill to amend the Licensing Act.

The main proposition the Government had to make was that the hours at which public-houses should be closed should be decided by statute, and not left to the discretion of the magistrates; on Sundays the hours should be left as fixed by Mr. Bruce (Lord Aberdare); in London, the week-day hours of closing should be 12.30 a.m., instead of midnight; in places of above 10,000 inhabitants, 11.30 p.m., instead of 11; and in the country the hour should remain at 11. Public opinion, however, was strong, and on going into Committee Mr. Cross stated that the Government were willing to make the hour of closing 11 p.m. in the provincial towns, instead of 11.30 as he had originally proposed, and 10 in the "pure country," instead of 11; but he retained the Metropolitan hour at 12.30 a.m., making a difference of an hour and a half, instead of Mr. Bruce's hour, in favour of the London publican. Under the former Act, the magistrates had it in their power to vary the hours of closing to some extent according to the special wants of their districts; but Mr. Cross, though he declared that "he threw overboard the principle of uniformity altogether," and ridiculed the publicans for what he called their "illogical" idea that the hours should be the same throughout the country, eventually adopted a more hard-and-fast line than his predecessor. In Cambridge, under the Licensing Act of 1872, the hour of closing was midnight; in Oxford, 11.30 p.m.; in Birmingham, 11 p.m.; and in Hull, 10.30 p.m.: Mr. Cross, in his detestation of the "illogical" principle of uniformity, closed them all at 11 p.m.

This was not a good beginning for the hopes of the publicans, and it betokened much of the vacillation that was to follow. The victuallers are not likely soon to forget their treatment on the Irish Sunday Closing Act, which is already quoted as a precedent for a similar measure to be applied to England. The manner in which, after opposing this, on the plea that it would create disorder and could not be safely or properly carried into effect, the Government swallowed the Bill and even assisted it, is not creditable to them, whether looked at from the view of the supporters or the opponents of the measure. It is a sinister omen for the publicans, as may be gathered from an incident which occurred in the House of Commons on March 11th of the present year. After Sir Wilfrid Lawson's " local option " resolution had been rejected, Mr. Serjeant Simon moved,—" That, in the opinion of this House, among the conditions prescribed by law for the granting of new licences for the sale of intoxicating liquors, it should be expressly provided that the licensing authority shall take into consideration the population and the number of existing licences in the district, and shall find as a fact, upon sworn evidence, that new licences are required for the necessary convenience of the public." Upon this Mr. Cross observed that though he did not say he agreed with the words of this amendment, he did with its principle, and therefore was prepared to support it. The licensed victuallers can form their own impression of what the effect of such a provision would be if application for a new licence had to be made to a bench of teetotal magistrates.

The Civil Servants.

Concerning the fourth section of the "harassed interests" of 1874, there is not so much to relate, for the all-sufficient reason that the Government has done nothing to redeem those promises to the Civil Service in which its members have occasionally indulged. Their delay in dealing with an acknowledged grievance being inexplicable, the attempts to explain it have failed to carry conviction to those most intimately concerned. The manner in which the Conservatives have promised reform and broken their pledge cannot be better put than in the following words from one of the aggrieved :—"In the year 1867 a memorial for inquiry into the anomalous position of the Customs Department was forwarded to the Treasury from the clerks and officers. The then Conservative Government spent a year in making this inquiry, and at the end of 1868, just on the eve of the dissolution of Parliament, a scheme was issued which was ordered to come into operation in the following April, when the Conservative Government had good reason to believe (and the fact did not belie it) that it would no longer be in office,— the natural result being that the scheme was immediately stopped by the new Treasury Board.

The conduct of the present Government, however, is far worse even than that of the last Conservative Administration. The most distinct promises of early settlement of the present question of reorganization have been made by successive Secretaries of the Treasury, only to be successively broken. Mr. W. H. Smith, Colonel Stanley, and Sir H. Selwin-Ibbetson have all in turn held out promises to the long-suffering officials of this department, and each in turn has failed to keep them." At the last election the civil servants voted almost to a man for Conservative candidates in the hope of favours to come; but though times have increased in hardness since 1874, no favours have they received.

No class of public servants, perhaps, has been so cruelly betrayed as the *employés* in the Government dockyards. In 1874, beguiled by the promises of the Tory candidates, every one of the dockyard towns rejected or degraded their Liberal representatives. Greenwich placed a distiller above Mr. Gladstone at the poll. Chatham turned out a tried and trusty servant for a Tory admiral, who received a comfortable command as a reward for his electioneering services. Portsmouth returned a Ministerialist, who sailed into a snug berth on the Treasury Bench, on the promises he made to the dockyard men, which remain unfulfilled to this day. And Devonport rejected an able and worthy representative, who had worked hard and honestly for his constituents, for a naval captain whose efforts in their behalf have been far from noteworthy. What have the dockyard *employés* gained by these changes? Have the mechanics received the promised increase of pay and continuous employment? Have the shipwrights who flocked into the dockyards in answer to the Government advertisements in the spring of 1878 been fairly treated? How many were discharged in the autumn, and how many old hands, who had been for eight, ten, or twelve years in the yard, were turned away with them? Have the clerks seen the flow of promotion which Ministerialist candidates pledged themselves to secure, and have they been placed on the same footing as the clerks in the Admiralty? How have the grievances of that most intelligent class of workmen, the engine-room artificers, been redressed? Two years ago an Admiralty Committee, specially appointed to inquire into their case, recommended certain ameliorations, which it declared ought to be effected as a matter of justice. Very few of these were even nominally adopted by the Government, and scarcely any have been carried out. An order, indeed, has been issued directing the engine-room artificers, alone of the civilian class of the chief petty officers, to wear a badge on their arms. But though they regard this badge as a symbol of servitude, and desire to get rid of it, no representations will induce the First Lord to recall the humiliating order. The Greenwich pensioners know whether the promises lavished upon them as to increase of pension at a reduced age have been performed. The whole body of mechanics are aware that many thousands of tons of shipping have been provided in private yards by the present Administration, and that millions of pounds sterling have been squandered outside, which under another Administration would have flowed inside the yards; while the small tradesmen in the dockyard towns who supply the wants of the fleet know that they have seen very little of the fleet during the last five years, as it has been generally in foreign waters, though they had promises from the Tory candidates in 1874 that, under a Tory Administration, it would be never, or hardly ever, outside the Channel. The dockyard towns have learned a bitter lesson, and one to be profited by on the day of reckoning.

III.—THE TORY POLICY AND THE PUBLIC PURSE.

"It is a very remarkable fact that there is always a difficulty in our foreign affairs."—Mr. Disraeli, *Debate on the Address*, February 3rd, 1857.

"It is a policy of perpetual meddling in every part of the world, occasioning disturbances which cause expense, and consequently lead to increased estimates. I am told that this is a very spirited policy, that there is nothing like making the influence of England felt, and that there is nothing of which an Englishman should be more proud than to feel that he is like a Roman citizen in every part of the world. . . How can you look forward to getting rid of the income tax unless you exercise strict control over the conduct of the Government with respect to interference in foreign countries?"—Mr. Disraeli, *Election Speech in Buckinghamshire*, April, 1857.

Among the many accusation brought against the Conservatives of late years, that of good financial management has never been numbered. Neither Mr. Disraeli, Mr. Ward Hunt, nor Sir Stafford Northcote has shown, as Chancellor of the Exchequer, such talent in dealing with his country's money as to be entitled to that country's gratitude. But this excuse is to be found for them all—that when they are in office "it is a very remarkable fact that there is always a difficulty in our foreign affairs." What with wars and rumours of wars, and the real or assumed necessity for increasing the armaments, the expenditure mounts up, deficits arise, and taxes increase. A policy begotten in strife and fed on extravagance is not likely to heighten the popularity of the Chancellor of the Exchequer who has to provide its cost.

Wars Threatened.

"What is this moral power to exercise which is now the policy of England ? . . . The consequence of the policy of what is called moral power—that is to say, warlike armaments in time of peace —of a dictatorial policy never conceding, scorning conciliation, shrinking from compromise, and never having forbearance—is that you find yourselves involved in war."—Mr. Disraeli, *Debate on the Customs and Inland Revenue Bill*, May 8th, 1862.

"I think it requires an unmistakable expression of feeling on the part of the nation before you can determine that its honour is concerned, and it requires on the part of the Minister great sagacity, great knowledge, and the possession of the highest qualities of a public man, before he can decide even that the interests of England are concerned in each case."—Mr. Disraeli, *Election Speech in Buckinghamshire*, July, 1865.

Russia, Burmah, and Egypt.

"I could settle the Eastern Question in a month, if I were disposed."—Mr. Disraeli *in* "*Tancred.*"

It would be hopeless to attempt in the space at disposal to give anything like a complete summary of the action of the Government on the Eastern Question. From the time of the outbreak in Bosnia and the Herzegovina in 1875, it has daily occupied the attention of the country, and a history of the whole proceedings would require volumes rather than pages. All that can be done is to indicate very briefly what might have been hoped from the past professions of members of the Government, and what has actually resulted.

After the events of the last two or three years it seems surprising to remember that the Ministry might have been expected to pursue a strictly non-interventionist course in foreign affairs. No one in times gone by has been more prominent in denouncing a "turbulent and aggressive" policy than the present Prime Minister. In the course of a speech in the House of Commons in April, 1864, Mr. Disraeli remarked that he thought at the time, and he thought so then, that the Crimean War was "unnecessary;" and this statement seems to be borne out by the fact that only a few hours before the outbreak of that conflict, he did not shrink, even at the risk of presenting the spectacle of a divided nation to the common enemy, from denouncing the conduct of the Aberdeen Government as having been marked "by vacillation, by perplexity, by fitfulness, by timidity, and by occasional violence." In 1859, in the debate on the Address, he made a still stronger statement in favour of non-intervention. "The general principle," he said, "that we ought not to interfere in the affairs of foreign nations unless there is a clear necessity, and that, generally speaking, it ought to be held a political dogma that the people of other countries should settle their own affairs without the introduction of foreign influence or foreign power, is one which I think the House does not only accept, but I trust will carefully adhere to. . . . . I ask them to contrast the position of England with that of any other country in the world. Has not the adhesion to the policy of non-interference by England been most beneficial? Has there ever been a period when England has occupied a prouder or more powerful position than that which she at present fills?" In a debate on Mr. Stansfeld's motion on the expenditure, in August, 1862, Mr. Disraeli declared that "we should hold aloof from that turbulent diplomacy which only distracts the mind of the people from internal improvement;" and in a Buckinghamshire election speech in July, 1865, he declared it to be "a fair boast for a Government if they can show that they have maintained the country at peace." And in this belief the Premier's first Foreign Secretary, Lord Derby, evidently shared; for in the course of a debate on our foreign relations in May,

1874, the noble Earl spoke as follows:—" It may be said that do what we may war will come sooner or later. I think it was Mr. Canning who in reply to a person who made a like remark to him, said, 'Well, if war is to come sooner or later, I should prefer that it would be rather later than sooner,'—and for the obvious reason that there is the chance that with time feelings of agitation will subside in men's minds, and that, therefore, there is the greater hope of the preservation of peace." When to these are added the strongly non-interventionist speeches of the Marquis of Salisbury before the Merchant Taylors in June, 1877, and before the people of Bradford in October of the same year, it might fairly have been expected that the Government would not have risked war (to use the words Mr. Disraeli once applied to Lord Palmerston's policy) " in the most rash and imprudent manner,—part and parcel, indeed, of a most rash and imprudent system."

And yet in our relations with Russia, war has again and again been risked without the country being distinctly aware of the point in dispute. Despite any indirect countenance which Lord Beaconsfield might give to Turkey by Guildhall speeches and ambassadorial appointments, Lord Salisbury plainly declared that the Government "were aware that it was no longer their duty to sustain the Turkish Empire by force of arms," and this should have served to remove any suspicion that the Ministry were wishful to rush into war. But the danger of drifting into strife has been with us ever since 1876, and cannot be said even yet to be removed, and still it has not been made clear which of our interests is at stake and what is the difficulty to be met. Vacillation has marked every step of our diplomacy; the acceptance of the Andrassy Note was followed by the rejection of the Berlin Memorandum; ostentatious indifference to the Bulgarian Atrocities was supplemented by an unenforced demand for the punishment of their perpetrators; the resolution, after the Constantinople Conference, to give no countenance to Turkey was succeeded by the appointment of a fanatically Turcophile ambassador; Lord Salisbury's despatch of defiance gave place to the Marvin Memorandum; the promise to aid Greece was fulfilled by allowing the Porte to deliberately delay a settlement; the declaration to literally abide by the Berlin Treaty was the prelude to suffering the Russians to postpone evacuation, and the Turks to abandon the Balkans. From first to last the same symptoms appear,—the Government vapours, vacillates, and is vanquished.

And what has been gained by such a course? The independence and integrity of the Ottoman Empire? Turkey has been " consolidated " by the loss of her richest provinces. The diminution of Russian influence? One Russian nominee rules Bulgaria, and another Eastern Roumelia. The fulfilment of treaties? That of Paris has been torn to shreds and that of Berlin promises an even shorter life. The defeat of Russia? Russia has more territory than ever. The concert of Europe? The Powers fail to agree in aught but disagreement. The honour of England? England is taunted on the Continent with having boasted at Berlin and succumbed at St. Petersburg. In what then has this policy of doubtful daring resulted? Gain to Russia, who was proclaimed as our foe; ruin to Turkey, who was announced as our friend; and debt, distress, and diplomatic defeat to ourselves, who should have been the first to be considered.

Whether such results are worth boasting of must be left to Ministerial orators defending the indefensible. We were told last July by the Prime Minister that " peace with honour " had been brought back from Berlin; we were told in May by the Foreign Secretary that the Treaty will be literally fulfilled; and the one assertion will bear as close inspection as the other. Peace had never been lost, honour had never left the banks of the Thames for those of the Spree; the literal fulfilment of the Treaty is already a myth; and all the declarations of Prime Minister or Foreign Secretary will not avail to falsify facts. When the story of this dispute is written—when the passion of to-day, skilfully inflamed by those in authority, has died into forgetfulness—the verdict of posterity will be, that in attempting to settle the Eastern Question by appealing to prejudice and neglecting principle, the Government of Lord Beaconsfield departed from England's traditional policy of succouring the weak and aiding the struggling, and used its strongest efforts to rivet the chains of oppression upon peoples longing to be free.

And as if this European imbroglio were not sufficient to satiate the Government with playing at Cæsarism, we have been threatened with complications in Asia and in Africa, additional to those in which we were already engaged. The organs which climb the Ministerial backstairs, and which may be thus supposed to write the opinions of their patrons, have advised war both with Burmah and with Egypt. In each case the object would be what in diplomacy is called annexation, and in commerce theft. In both countries the monarch offends our sensibilities by cruelty or extortion; and to prevent the possibility of either potentate doing us some undefined injury at a future time, we are asked to invade the territories of both without delay. What is to be gained by all this, but further loss of British life, is not apparent; not even the most hungry seeker after national glory can pretend that England would earn any honour from crushing such wretched foes. Imperialism must have sunk low when it retreats before Alexander and bullies Theebaw.

But the opinion of the people, little as it has weighed with the present Government, is becoming too strong to tolerate an attack on Burmah at the bidding of enterprising Bombay merchants, or upon Egypt at that of disinterested bondholders. Filibustering, disguised as anxiety for scientific frontiers, or the spread of the Gospel, may pass muster for a time, but there is a limit to a nation's patience, and that is reached when the desire to obtain a new trading station or the payment of an old debt is the avowed reason for launching the country into war. There is, it is to be hoped, as little reason now to fear war with Burmah or with Egypt as there is with Russia, but it cannot be forgotten how near we have been to it with each, and that had not the people exercised their undoubted but frequently denied right of criticising the Government's foreign policy, we might now have had five wars on our hands instead of one.

Wars Commenced.

"He who involves his country in interference or in war under the idea that the interests or honour of the country are concerned, when neither is substantially involved—he who involves his country in interference or war because he believes the independence of Europe is menaced, when, in fact, the independence of Europe is not in danger—makes, of course, a great, a fatal mistake."—Mr. Disraeli, *Debate on the Address*, 1858.

"Let us be quite sure, if we go to war, first of all that it is a necessary and just war; and secondly, if now necessary, whether it might not have been prevented by more astute and skilful management."—Mr. Disraeli, *Debate on the Address*, 1864.

Afghan and Zulu.

"In an age accused, and perhaps not unjustly, of selfishness and a too great regard for material interests, it is something for a great nation to have vindicated the higher principles of humanity."—Mr. Disraeli, *Vote of thanks to the Abyssinian Forces*, July 2nd, 1868.

"If the power of declaring war and peace was left entirely in the hands of the Sovereign in India, there were not the means of controlling its exercise that existed in this country, and a policy might be pursued entirely injurious to the national interests."—Mr. Disraeli *on the Government of India Bill*, July 6th, 1858.

It would be well if we had only to consider wars threatened; but unfortunately for British prestige, we have to glance at wars commenced, neither of which redounds to the credit of the nation. In Afghanistan we have been and in Zululand we are slaughtering our hundreds of natives, partly, according to the Government's episcopal supporters and Sir Bartle Frere, to propagate the Gospel, and mostly, according to Lord Beaconsfield, to improve our frontier and secure our possessions. The Afghan campaign has terminated, at least for a time; but Cetewayo is of different calibre to Yakoob, and the raiding in Zululand may drag its length along until many more men are lost to England,—many more than those who already lie on the fields of Isandula, Kambula, and Gingihlova.

Whatever the Afghan dispute may end in, the proceedings of Parliament will prove that it had its origin in truth suppressed and falsehood suggested. In November, 1875, the Marquis of Salisbury directed Lord Northbrook, the then Viceroy (whose policy, like that of previous Viceroys, was not to harass the Ameer), to "find, or, if need be, to create," a pretext for pressing a mission on Shere Ali. Lord Northbrook's creative faculty was not equal to Lord Salisbury's demands, and Lord Lytton was sent to India to show that a poet could falsify where a politician could fail. Granted "every reasonable freedom" in carrying out his instructions, Lord Lytton lost little time in manufacturing the required excuse for coercing Shere Ali; for on May 10th, 1876, he informed Lord Salisbury that he and his Council "were of opinion that the opportunity and pretext hitherto wanting for the despatch of a complimentary special mission to Cabul, were furnished by His Excellency's recent accession to office, and the addition which the Queen had been pleased to make to Her Sovereign titles with special regard to India." They accordingly "made immediate preparations for announcing these events to Shere Ali;" and in order to secure, if possible, a friendly reception of the Mission, a trusted native officer was deputed, in the first instance, to deliver to the Ameer a letter containing its "ostensible objects." But the Ameer saw through the pretext, and declined to receive the Mission, whereupon hostile letters were sent to him, and he ultimately agreed to receive the British agent. The terms offered to the Ameer were either that he should assent to the location of British officers in Afghanistan, or that all assistance from the British Government would be withdrawn, and, "yielding to necessity," Shere Ali agreed to open negotiations on that basis. These negotiations were carried on between the Prime Minister of the Ameer and Sir Lewis Pelly at Peshawur, in February, 1877; and the Viceroy instructed Sir Lewis to ask the Prime Minister whether he was directed by the Ameer to refuse to entertain any proposal for the residence of British officers in Afghanistan. Owing to the death of the Minister, no answer was returned to this; and the Viceroy immediately ordered the Conference to be closed, though the Indian Government, in their despatch to Lord Salisbury, say that "at the moment when Sir L. Pelly was closing the Conference, a fresh envoy was already on the way from Cabul to Peshawur, and it was reported that this envoy had authority to accept, eventually, all the conditions of the British Government. The Viceroy was aware of these facts when he instructed our envoy to close the Conference." Such conduct, as was only to be expected, intensified Shere Ali's bitterness towards England; and it is in this Conference that the proximate cause of the war is to be found. In a despatch of May 10th, 1877, Lord Lytton reported the issue of the Conference to Lord Salisbury; and with the judicial calmness of utterance always characteristic of his despatches, deals with the plea for delay by the Ameer on the ground of illness as a "transparent pretext," which "the [British] Vakeel, either from stupidity or disloyalty, accepted." With this despatch in his hands, Lord Salisbury did not hesitate to state in the House of Lords, on June 15th, 1877, that the Government had not tried to force an envoy upon the Ameer, that their relations with the Ameer had undergone no material change, and that there was no reason for any apprehension of any change of policy, or of disturbance to our Indian Empire. And Sir Stafford Northcote, two months later, not only added to this in the House of Commons that the main lines of their policy were unchanged, but demurred to the idea that the best way to meet danger was to advance beyond our own frontier. So matters smouldered; Lord Salisbury grew more confident in Lord Lytton, Lord Lytton more antagonistic towards Shere Ali, and Shere Ali more suspicious of the British Government; and matters tended rapidly to a crisis. During June and July of last year, Lord Lytton, probably noting the effect Mr. Layard's alarmist telegrams of a few months previous had had upon the Ministry, forwarded several on his own account. On June 7th, the visit of a Russian envoy to Cabul was impending; on June 18th, the Ameer was being pressed to receive an important Russian Embassy; and on July 30th and 31st, the modern edition of the "three black crows," in the shape of a similar number of Russians, was reported to have reached Cabul. Lord Cranbrook, who was now in Lord Salisbury's place, appears, at the first, not to have reposed such implicit confidence as his predecessor in the Viceroy's information and judgment, and curtly telegraphed to Lord Lytton: "Make yourself certain of the facts before insisting on the reception of British envoy," that being the course suggested from India. Telegram succeeded telegram, and despatch followed despatch, until the formation of Sir Neville Chamberlain's Mission to Cabul. Our native envoy recommended postponing its advance, in consequence of the death of the Ameer's favourite son; but this kind of "transparent pretext," which the native, "either from stupidity or disloyalty," sympathised with, had no weight with Lord Lytton, who ordered the Mission to proceed. In asking the Viceroy's authority to make arrangements with the Khyber tribes for the safety of the Mission, Sir Neville Chamberlain warned Lord Lytton that "it should be clearly understood that our doing this will be viewed by the Ameer as an act of hostility;" but the preparations for invasion went on. On September 21st, the Mission was refused passage through the Khyber Pass; and on October 19th, Shere Ali's answer to the Viceroy's communication was received, saying, "I am astonished and dismayed by this letter, written threateningly to a well-intentioned friend, replete with contentions, and yet nominally regarding a friendly Mission. Coming thus by force, what result, or profit, or fruit could come of it? . . . Looking to the fact that I am at this time assaulted by affliction and grief at the hand of Fate, and that great trouble had possessed my soul, in the officials of the British Government, patience and silence would have been specially becoming. . . . There is some difference between this and the pure road of friendship and goodwill." The Viceroy did not appreciate such home thrusts, and without a day's delay telegraphed to Lord Cranbrook: "Any demand for apology would now, in my opinion, be useless, and only expose us to fresh insult, while losing valuable time." Three or four hours later, he despatched another telegram urging the immediate declaration of war, "fixing sole responsibility on Ameer;"

adding, "advantages of delay, none; disadvantages, obvious;" to which, six days afterwards, Lord Cranbrook replied: "Do not consider matters to be at present ripe for taking all the steps you mention," and directed that, before crossing the frontier, an ultimatum, "in temperate language," should be issued. This was done, and the result was war, the *casus belli* alleged being the reception by the Ameer of a Russian envoy "at a time when a war was believed to be imminent, in which England and Russia would have been arrayed on opposite sides," and the subsequent repulse of a British Mission. Whatever justification may be found in the latter pretext (to use a word with which both Lord Salisbury and Lord Lytton have made us familiar), the worth of the former may be guessed from the fact that whereas the Salisbury-Schouvaloff Memorandum, sacrificing Turkey to Russia, and thus destroying the probability of a war between England and the latter power, was signed at the end of May, the Russian Embassy is not alleged, even by the Viceroy, to have reached Cabul before the end of July, a fortnight after Lord Beaconsfield had assured the English public that "peace with honour" had been secured. It is on a par for veracity with the Premier's Guildhall statement, at once contradicted by Lord Northbrook, that the question of the frontier had been brought before previous Viceroys.

The strange character of official pleas is as strongly marked in connection with the Zulu as with the Afghan War. Sir Bartle Frere, whose letter to the late Sir John Kaye, of June 12th, 1874, recommending that "something should be done," contributed greatly to the attack upon the Ameer, has followed in Africa the policy he formulated for India. Our troubles with Cetewayo are of later growth than those with Shere Ali, but have already had more disastrous effects, and, to put it at the mildest, Sir Bartle Frere's chances of future preferment are seriously compromised by the fact that his policy has brought us into war in two of the positions in which he has been most prominent. That Cetewayo has not always been deemed a foe may be gathered from official testimony of recent date. Sir Henry Bulwer, the Lieutenant-Governor of Natal, writing on November 15th, 1875, refers to the "peace and goodwill" which for thirty years have been maintained between the British Government and the Zulus, though "separated for more than a hundred miles of border line by only a stream of water, both banks of which are occupied to the water's edge by the subjects respectively of the two Governments." Writing to Cetewayo on January 25th, 1876, Sir Henry Bulwer expresses "the pleasure with which he has heard of the satisfactory relations that have always existed between the colony and the Zulus." And on September 4th of the same year, Sir Henry states his belief that Cetewayo would do nothing that would "lessen the good opinion which his conduct, since he ascended the Zulu throne, has gained for him in the eyes of the great Queen." And on December 8th, 1877, only eighteen months since, he describes the relations of the English and the Zulus as "having always been friendly." But the annexation of the Transvaal, however it may be justified on many grounds, indirectly changed all this. The Boers had had land disputes with Cetewayo, the rights of which, as long as the Transvaal was independent, seemed to most English administrators to be on the side of the Zulus. But with annexation, the English officials adopted the views of the Boers, and to this are to be traced our late disasters. The Zulus, who had previously been considered to be standing only on their rights, were now treated as annoyances, though, as Sir Henry Bulwer pointed out to Sir Bartle Frere on August 12th,

1878, "we must not forget that, if the action of the Zulus has of late been of an aggressive character, it is aggression by those who hold themselves to be aggrieved, and that it has been in vindication of Zulu rights suffering injury from alleged Transvaal aggression." The land question grew into a quarrel, which Sir Bartle Frere had the power but not the will to settle, for on the same day that he forwarded to Cetewayo his award in this matter, and which, while professing to cede the Zulu claim, took away with one hand what it gave with the other, he sent an ultimatum (issued because of an outrage which two of the sons and a brother of Sirayo, a powerful chief, committed in Natal in July of last year), not only asking the surrender of the offenders, and 500 head of cattle, but making further demands, which the course of the war will show that Cetewayo had great ground for believing himself to be justified in refusing. The king was called upon to disband his army; to agree never to call out his troops for war, or to assemble them in regiments, except with the permission of the British Government, as well as of the Great Council of the Zulus; to permit every man to marry on coming to man's estate; to secure a fair trial to all offenders; to allow the missionaries to return and re-occupy their stations; to surrender Umbelini; and to receive a British Resident, who should have joint authority with the king in all disputes concerning Europeans. That Cetewayo should have been asked to disband within thirty days such an army as his has proved to be, was an insult to his understanding; that England should be called upon to spread the Bible by bloodshed, and support missions by the Martini-Henry, is an insult to ours. Sir Bartle's pill to cure every earthquake, the pill he wished to administer first to Shere Ali and then to Cetewayo,—the appointment of a British Resident,—is about as valuable, and has proved as likely to be swallowed, as his demand for the surrender of Umbelini—an independent chief, who proved his prowess in engagements with General Wood—was reasonable and possible to be acceded to. Sir Bartle's self-asserted sympathy with aboriginal races did not serve to save the Zulu king from demands excessive to the degree of absurdity, nor would it have served—had not public opinion proved once more too strong for the Ministry—to save the Zulu nation from practical extinction. If the Ex-High Commissioner's declaration to the Boers that the English never recede from a point over which their flag has once waved, be correctly reported, it is evident that he was prepared to treat the avowed instructions of the Government not to annex territory as lightly as he treated their published censure.

And this brings us to the consideration of how the Government at home has dealt with those agents abroad who have brought England into disastrous contests. Though Lord Cranbrook on more than one occasion treated Lord Lytton's frantic appeals for immediate action with a coolness resembling contempt, confidence is still expressed in the Viceroy, and the popular demand for his recall is neglected. And though Sir Michael Hicks-Beach censured Sir Bartle Frere as no man of honour and spirit would have submitted to be censured without resigning, the High Commissioner retained his post until the popular demand for his dismissal became too strong to be withstood. The passport to Government approval seemed the manufacture of a new war, and a peaceful administrator was looked on as pusillanimous. But the vigour displayed in finding fresh pretexts for strife is far in advance of that shown in bringing such strife to a victorious conclusion. The Afghan War dragged along in a half-hearted fashion, which, according to the

Times, sickened both officers and men with the whole business, until at Gundamak a peace was patched up containing all the elements of future strife. The Zulu War, undermanned from the first, will require further and frequent reinforcements. In March, 1874, in proposing a vote of thanks to the British troops who had just returned from the victorious campaign in Ashantee, the Prime Minister said,—" In the middle of that month [October, 1873] he [Sir Garnet Wolseley] wrote to the Government [that of Mr. Gladstone], and informed them that the business could not be done without British troops. That appeal of Sir Garnet Wolseley was answered by Her Majesty's Government with laudable promptitude. Not a moment was lost in giving orders that some of the flower of the English army should be despatched to that part of the world." If it fall to the lot, as a general election may cause it to do, of Mr. Gladstone to propose the vote of thanks to the British troops returned from Zululand, could he, with the least truthfulness, use similar expressions? Some of the apologists of the Ministry have urged that they failed in their duty of sending sufficient troops because, had they increased the number of soldiers, they would have been blamed by the

Opposition on the ground of expense. That this, in addition to being a purely gratuitous assumption, is a weak defence for a powerful Government, goes for the saying. But those who profess to imitate Lord Palmerston's foreign policy should take the following to heart :—" It is the duty of a responsible Government, having determined the amount of army and navy which is essential for the safety and interest of the country, to present to Parliament the result of the conclusions to which they have arrived." * The fact is, the present Government wished the luxury of playing at a " spirited foreign policy" without the loss of popularity consequent upon paying for it; and the first result of ill-timed parsimony, in conjunction with reckless administration and incompetent generalship, was the defeat of Isandula.

ACCUMULATED EXPENDITURE AND INCREASED TAXATION.

Sir Stafford Northcote's Six Budgets.

"The state of our finances is most critical, and our financial prospects are dark and dubious."—MR. DISRAELI *on the Palmerston Administration*, August 1st, 1862.

"How he became Chancellor of the Exchequer, and how the Government to which he belonged became a Government, it would

* *Debate on the Address*, 1857.

be difficult to tell. Like flies in amber, 'one wondered how the devil they got there.'"—Mr. Disraeli *on Mr. Fox Maule*, July 24th, 1839.

"We have had a war expenditure in time of peace, combined, and erroneously combined, with a system of finance that only a peace expenditure could justify. . . . When his financial embarrassments commence, he is perfectly ready to draw upon posterity. He is establishing a precedent which, if sanctioned by the House, will allow him to engage the expenditure of the country in worthless purposes of any sort with impunity."—Mr. Disraeli *on the Palmerston Administration*, June 23rd, 1862.

Sir Stafford Northcote is personally so pleasant that it is to be regretted for his sake that so little can be said in favour of his financial experiments. With a splendid opportunity for winning the gratitude of at least some sections of the community, he has secured the thanks of none, and bids fair rapidly to earn the distrust of all. A Chancellor of the Exchequer who adds to the expenditure, raises taxation, and draws bills upon the future, can hardly be considered a success, and the history of Sir Stafford Northcote's six budgets is a lamentable tale of surpluses shrinking into deficits, and promises to remit changed into proposals to increase the taxation of the country. In the Budget of 1874, with the surplus of six millions which had been left by Mr. Gladstone, Sir Stafford reduced the Income Tax a penny, abolished the duties on sugar, horses, and horse-dealers, and set aside half-a-million towards the extinction of the National Debt; the aggregate total of these various reductions bringing the original surplus down to £462,000, this being the available margin between revenue and expenditure which the Budget proposed to retain. In 1875, Sir Stafford found himself in the position of having neither deficiency to meet, nor substantial surplus to dispose of. In the year the expenditure had been £75,268,000 and the revenue £75,685,000, and with this trifling balance in hand he proposed to throw a sop to the brewers over their licences, and to establish a sinking fund. In order to justify the latter proposition, Sir Stafford calculated upon an annual surplus of £500,000 for the next thirty years. "Why," exclaimed Mr. Gladstone, in the course of the debate, "if he had a surplus of £500,000 himself to begin with, there would be some spark of comfort in viewing the scheme; but he has not a farthing of surplus." The Bill for establishing a sinking fund was carried in the teeth of sharp opposition, but before the end of the session supplementary estimates had been proposed to an amount which made a deficit of what the Chancellor hinted would be a surplus. Thus, as far back as 1875,

Sir Stafford had commenced that system of extensive supplementary estimates which has made the Budget statement a mere delusion, the whole of its calculations being upset before the end of the session. The Budget for 1876 was by no means rose-coloured. Sir Stafford asserted that the surplus was £710,000, but destroyed the effect of this by adding that the next year's expenditure (£78,044,000) would exceed the estimated revenue by £800,000. With this prospect he intended raising the Income Tax a penny, with some extra exemptions, preferring this mode to adding to the Spirit Duties, and calculating that by this means he should change his deficit into a surplus of £368,000. Twelve months later Sir Stafford stated that the actual surplus exceeded his expectation, and was really £443,000, and he estimated that that for the next year would be £226,000, the revenue being £79,020,000, and the expenditure £78,794,044. This state of things, according to the Chancellor, presented him with a "ready-made Budget," it being clear that there was no necessity to add to the taxation of the country, nor was it possible to take any tax off, and this Sir Stafford flattered himself was "safe," though admitting that it was not "brilliant." Twelve months later the Chancellor stated that, generally speaking, the revenue had turned out very satisfactorily, having produced £617,298 more than he had anticipated, the surplus being £859,803; but £3,500,000 had been spent within the year out of the Vote of Credit, which converted the surplus into a deficit of £2,640,000. To supply this £750,000 had been taken from the ordinary surplus of the year, and £2,750,000 had been raised by Exchequer Bonds for one year. Calculating that his next year's revenue would be £79,460,000, the Chancellor reckoned his expenditure at £81,019,676, leaving him with a prospective deficit of, roundly speaking, £1,560,000. which was to be partly met by an increase on the Dog Tax and the Tobacco Duty, and an extra twopence on the Income Tax. In his Budget statement for 1879, the Chancellor was forced to confess that all his prognostications of sufficient revenue from increased taxation had been falsified. The revenue had only been £83,115,972 instead of the estimated £83,230,000, whilst the expenditure had been £85,407,789, which was an addition of £4,388,000 to the original estimates. In place, therefore, of the surplus he had anticipated, varying from £750,000 to £1,250,000, he found himself with a deficit of £2,291,817, and none of the Exchequer Bonds had been paid off as promised. For 1879-80 he estimated his expenditure to be £81,153,573, and his revenue £83,055,000, showing a surplus for the coming year of £1,900,000, excluding any future charge for the South African War and the repayment of the Exchequer Bonds. The outstanding bonds amounted to £4,750,000; but after dwelling on the inexpediency of increasing taxes, and the mischievous alternative of adding the deficit to the funded debt, he announced his preference for the *viâ media* of spreading the payment of the bonds over one year more, and authority would, at the proper time, be taken for paying £2,000,000 in 1880, and the remaining £2,750,000 in 1881. The criticisms which have been bestowed upon this latest development of Conservative financial policy have shown its dangerous and even dishonest tendency. It palms upon the people as a fact that which the initiated know to be a fiction, and throws upon the future that which the present ought of right to bear. The fireworks have been shown and the bill is heavy, and the latter consideration, as involving probable loss of popularity and power, is held to be sufficient by a Conservative Government to justify placing the cost upon the taxpayers of some years hence, who will neither have approved nor derived benefit from the policy for which they will have to pay.

Tory and Liberal Finance.

"I believe there is no instance of a well-considered measure of retrenchment which has not been carried into effect by the Tory party; and . . . the Tory party will never forget that it is they who were the original opponents of any extravagantly-conceived military establishments of this country."—Mr. Disraeli, *Debate on the Address*, February 1st, 1849.

A comparison between the finance of the five years of Liberal plenty and that of the five years of Tory famine is not only interesting, but most important at the present time. The total expenditure of 1872-3, the last year in which the Liberal Government had its exclusive control, was £70,714,000; that of 1878-79, the last, it may be expected, in which the Conservative Government will have its exclusive control, was £85,407,789; and making the fairest deductions, the balance in favour of the Liberals is fourteen millions. The expenditure having increased at an average of nearly three millions yearly since the Conservatives entered power, it may fairly be asked where it is likely to stop. It is true that Sir Stafford Northcote estimates the expenditure of the coming twelve months at only £81,153,573, but seeing that the cost of the Zulu War is not included, and that this threatens to go on for some considerable time, it is unlikely that the sum mentioned will anything like resemble that which will have to be announced in the next Budget. The practical effect of five Liberal Budgets was to remit taxes to the amount of £12,951,000, to reduce the Debt by £26,200,000, and to leave their successors a surplus of at least £5,500,000; the practical effect of the first five Conservative Budgets (and if the sixth were added it would make it look worse for the party in power) was to impose taxes to the amount of £5,233,000 over the amount remitted, to reduce the Debt (in four years) by only £1,500,000, and to create a deficit of £4,300,000. This is a state of things which must come home to every taxpayer.

Deficit and Distress.

"What is the real state of affairs at present? The distress in this country is very great."—Lord Beaconsfield, *Debate on the Address*, December 5th, 1878.

And not only is it a state of things to trouble the mind and burden the pocket of every taxpayer, but it is one to bear hardly on a struggling people already heavily weighted by trade-depression. The stagnation of commerce which has troubled most civilised countries during the past few years is not to be traced to one cause or one set of causes, but few will doubt that the warlike movements at home and abroad have deepened the distress. At a time when any moment might plunge the nation into conflict, enterprise could not be expected in those departments of trade to the full development of which peace is necessary. Manufacturers of guns and armour, tents and ambulances, might thrive while others starved; but unproductive work of that character could do little to retrieve the falling fortunes of the commercial classes and those who depend upon them for a livelihood. In these categories are to be included the vast majority of the people; and repeated war-panics have seriously retarded that return of trade which alone could bring back bread to the hungry. It was many years since that such distress was to be seen in England as that recently witnessed. Pooh-poohed by members of the Government, it had to be alleviated by public subscription, and town after town had to form relief committees to save from starvation despairing thousands. This state of things would have been bad enough with the national finances in good order; but when, from frequent incitements to war, taxation has had to be increased instead of remitted, it becomes an additional grinding force upon those already suffering too much. Deficit has not caused, but it has intensified distress; trade can only revive with the return of a peaceful policy and sound finance.

IV.—FAILURES, FIASCOES, AND FABLES.

"If you borrow your political ethics from the ethics of the political adventurer, you may depend upon it that the whole of your representative institutions will crumble beneath your feet. . . . Even if I deemed [this policy] to be most advantageous, I should still regret to find that the House of Commons had applauded a policy of legerdemain."—VISCOUNT CRANBORNE (now the MARQUIS OF SALISBURY) *on the Derby-Disraeli Ministry,* July 15th, 1867.

When the present Premier met Parliament in 1874, after the formation of his Ministry, he must have felt a strong satisfaction with the prospect before him. Possessed of a compact majority, supported by a "safe" Cabinet, confronted by a disorganised Opposition, he seemed to have everything his own way—the present was smiling and the future smooth. It is curious to note how soon the clouds gathered in this pleasant sky. Legislative projects failed to meet support, administrative proposals managed to win ridicule, and Ministerial assertions proved to be false. The members of the Government enveloped themselves in mistakes and mis-statements, and, while rallying the Opposition to battle, lost supporters throughout the country. In June, 1874, the average politician would not have taken odds against the Conservatives holding office for another ten years; in June, 1879, he would give odds against their holding it for another ten months. What has caused this revolution in public sentiment? What but failures, fiascoes, and fables?

Legislative Failures.

"It seems to me a barren thing, this Conservatism, an unhappy cross-breed; the mule of politics that engenders nothing."—Mr. Disraeli *in* "*Coningsby.*"

For those who have the necessary leisure, it would be an interesting study to go through the Parliaments of the past half-century and try to find one as barren as the present. For a full five sessions and the most of a sixth, have its members assembled and filled Westminster with the noise of debate and the rush of division, and during the whole time no measure of first-rate importance has been placed upon the statute-book. Granting that there was no reason to expect any repetition of the "heroic legislation" of the last House, we have a right to ask the outcome of the promised programme, *Sanitas sanitatum omnia sanitas*. Though the Government has been as seemingly busy at home as it has been seemingly brave abroad, the result of the one has been as permissive as that of the other has been submissive, and neither has been worth the trouble and the cost.

Abortive Projects.

In the first session of the present Parliament, the Ministry introduced more than one measure which has failed in its avowed intention. The Scotch Church Patronage Bill, to take one of the earliest, had for its object the abolition of the system of lay patronage in the Established Kirk, and the making it over to the congregation, the Government's belief being that the contemplated measure would give renewed strength and vitality to the Establishment. This seemed also the view of the House of Lords, where it might almost be said to have been "carried with acclamation;" but in the House of Commons the welcome was scarcely so warm. There Mr. Baxter moved an amendment declaring it inexpedient to legislate without further inquiry and information.

In this he was supported by Mr. Gladstone, who wanted to know what the General Assembly had done towards re-uniting itself to bodies which, holding the view which formed the basis of the Bill, it turned out; and he added: "There was scarcely any Disestablishment movement in Scotland until the introduction of this, I do not call it bad, but crude, premature, and insufficiently considered Bill. But is it true that there is no promise of a Disestablishment movement in Scotland now? What has happened since the announcement of this Bill? The representatives of 1,200,000 of the Scottish people have in their General Assembly declared for Disestablishment . . . by a very large majority, for the first time in their history." Mr. Gladstone's prophecy that the measure would intensify a Disestablishment movement it assisted to create has been fulfilled, as is evident from the warmth and assiduity with which the claims of that cause are now being pushed among the constituencies of Scotland.

To the utter incompetence of the Public Worship Regulation Act to put down Ritualism, reference has already been made; and a Judicature Bill of the same session, designed to abolish the appellate jurisdiction of the House of Lords, had to be withdrawn, and was defeated the next year by a Conservative "caucus" movement of the most pronounced type. In 1875, also, the Chancellor of the Exchequer shared with the Lord Chancellor the mortification of defeat. Sir Stafford Northcote introduced a Bill dealing with Savings Banks, which was read a second time, at one in the morning, without discussion, and without a division. On going into Committee, however, Mr. Gladstone characterised the measure as "a mere device, not so intended, but in its effect, for hiding from Parliament and the country the clumsy, unworkmanlike, and highly impolitic nature of the scheme." One night, and one night only, the Bill struggled in Committee, during the discussion in which Mr. Disraeli expressed his "trust that the Committee will, in a manner which cannot be mistaken, sanction our policy, and satisfy those who are our fellow-subjects, and are deeply interested in this question, that their just interests will be guarded and preserved by the present Government." The Committee did what was asked, but from that night forth nothing was heard of the Bill. Some of the most important clauses had been abandoned at an early stage, and the measure was ultimately dropped without further debate. In the next year Mr. Sclater-Booth succeeded in doing that which Lord Salisbury had failed to do in 1875—namely, in passing a Pollution of Rivers Bill. It was, however, of so weak a nature, owing to the concessions made to the manufacturing interest, that it was scarcely worth the passing; and Mr. Booth himself admitted that it was in some respects a skeleton Bill, and that thereafter it might be necessary to make other regulations.

But the sanitary success, such as it was, of 1876, was not emulated by the Duke of Richmond's attempt in a professedly similar direction in 1877. In presenting the Burials Act Consolidation Bill to the House of Lords, the noble Duke declared that the measure proposed to treat the Burials Question in a sanitary point of view. It was true that a clause had been introduced to provide for the Dissenters' difficulty by allowing silent burial, but this was not mentioned until late in the speech, because His Grace preferred, so he said, to rest his case on sanitary and consolidation grounds. The Upper House appeared so pleased with the measure, that clauses 1 to 73 inclusive were agreed to without discussion, and there only remained to be passed the one dealing with the religious point.

But over this a great fight took place, ending in the defeat of the Government by the insertion of the Earl of Harrowby's clause allowing at the grave other Christian and orderly services than those of the Church of England. Then the Duke declared that the amendment was "so opposed to the general scheme of the Bill, and would so entirely disarrange the principle on which it was founded," that it was incumbent on the Cabinet to withdraw it, and this though the case rested on "sanitary and consolidation grounds," and the clauses dealing with these grounds had been passed without division.

A more successful measure of the session of 1877, in point of passage, though as little useful as if it had shared a like fate, was the Act which was designed to suppress the "Colorado beetle." By the provisions of this measure, specimens of the far-famed insect, when found, were to be made a note of, and carried to the nearest policeman, who would have to forward it to the Privy Council. For some weeks after this became law, harmless beetles of all kinds were captured and sent to London, their full description being meanwhile telegraphed all over the country; but, as far as is generally known, all the powers of the Privy Council were of no avail in effecting the seizure of a single genuine specimen on English soil. Mr. Sclater-Booth's attempts to provide a satisfactory County Board have proved as fruitless as the Duke of Richmond's to catch a Colorado beetle. Forced by circumstances to promise in 1877 to do something, his proposal of 1878 died a natural death, and that of 1879 has been strangled in its cradle.

As if all the prominent Ministers should be able to controvert the first Lord Lytton's assertion that "there's no such word as fail," Mr. Cross, in obedience to promise, introduced in 1878 a Bill proposing to appoint a Scotch Under-Secretaryship of State. The second reading being moved without a word, Mr. Cross was asked to furnish some statement to show what was meant by the Bill, to which he replied that the whole thing was fully explained, as far as the principle was concerned, when he asked for leave to introduce the Bill. This was proved to be a mistake, not a single word having been said on the subject when it was brought in. Mr. Cross's answer was ingenious: "Technically, he might have been wrong in saying that when he introduced the Bill he explained fully its object. On that occasion he might have got up and simply said that the Bill would carry out what he had stated the night before. The whole thing, however, was fully explained." And Mr. Cross declining to give any further account of the measure, it was read a second time and committed. Further than that stage it never advanced, for it was subsequently withdrawn without remark.

Permissive Bills.

It is probable that one of the principal objections the occupants of the Treasury Bench have towards Sir Wilfrid Lawson's Permissive Bill is that it includes the word "Prohibitory" in its title, and there is so little that is prohibitory in the permissive bills they carry, that the feeling may be understood. So much has been claimed for the Artizans' Dwellings Act of 1875, one of the most notable specimens of a Conservative permissive bill, that it would be interesting to have a Parliamentary return, showing how many and what towns have adopted its provisions. Domestic legislation being a prominent inscription on the modern Conservative banner, it might have been thought that this measure at least would have been so designed as to be generally useful; but the limitations were so many and the facilities of operation so few that its effect has been practically *nil*. It is true that corporations (and only these in boroughs of over twenty-five thousand inhabitants) can, under its provisions, acquire buildings by compulsory purchase for the purpose of improvement, and may either build or let the land for building, with special regard for the working classes; but any municipality wishing to do this had all the opportunity previously by means of private Acts, and the additional gain to them is difficult to perceive. It is known that at Birmingham the Act has been put fully into operation, and it is believed that in one or two other places houses have been knocked down under its provisions. But as these have not been put up again, the advantage to the artizan is not obvious, and very little benefit is to be expected from the measure until more stringency is put into its operations.

The Agricultural Holdings Act and the Friendly Societies Act come into the same category, though the latter has been of more use than the former, because those affected by it have been more ready to take advantage of it than the landlords have been to grant a measure of justice to their tenants. For scarcely any but members of the Ministry now deny that the permissive character of the Agricultural Holdings Act has been fatal to its value; and seeing that at least one prominent occupant of the Cabinet (whom rumour asserts to be identical with the introducer of the measure), and a Government department contract themselves out of its provisions, it is not to be wondered at that among the Ministerial failures this is one of the most prominent.

Reactionary Measures.

In the Endowed Schools Act Amendment Bill of 1874, the Government first showed their deliberate desire to be reactionary. The measure, as introduced by Lord Sandon, proposed to transfer to the Charity Commissioners the powers then held by the Endowed Schools Commissioners appointed by the Act of 1869, and to alter the definitions contained in the former Act, so as to restore to the Established Church the administration of a number of schools then open to Nonconformists as well. The vital change introduced by the Government lost nothing of its force in Lord Sandon's oratorical assault upon the Nonconformists; and Mr. Forster, the sponsor of the previous Act, moved the rejection of the Bill because it was retrograde and unfair, its mutations of policy unwise and unjust, and its changes in administration unnecessary and inexpedient. Mr. Gladstone added his testimony that the measure was inequitable, unusual, and unwise, and pointed to the remarkable fact that the Conservative majority were about to undo an Act they never opposed in its passage. Nevertheless the second reading was carried by a majority of eighty-two, which was reduced, however, to sixty-one upon an amendment on going into committee, moved by Mr. Fawcett, and declaring the inexpediency of sanctioning a measure which would allow any one religious body to control schools that had been thrown open to the whole nation by the policy of the previous Parliament. Learning wisdom by experience, the Chancellor of the Exchequer endeavoured to tone down the rough places raised by Lord Sandon, suggesting that alterations for the better could be made in committee, and after two nights' further warfare Mr. Disraeli announced the abandonment of the Foundation Clauses, and the restriction of the measure to the mere transfer of the powers of the Endowed Schools Commissioners to the Charity Commissioners. In doing this the right hon. gentleman noticed the fact that the disputed clauses had given rise to great differences of opinion as to their construction and meaning, and declared that, although the confession might seem to prove his incapacity to fill the position he occupied, he must admit that, after hours of anxious consideration, the clauses were unintelligible to him. He had accepted them on the faith of "the adepts and experts" to whom he had looked for instruction in such matters; they had failed him, and the meaning of these clauses of his own Bill was obscure and hidden from his comprehension, and they would therefore be withdrawn. Mr. Disraeli, in a previous speech, had claimed the Bill as the Bill of the Cabinet, and as prepared by the Ministers in common, and now he threw all the blame of the reactionary portions upon the draughtsman, who was not present to speak for himself. But whatever they might think of such an apology for such a policy, the Liberals had gained their main end, though Mr. Disraeli's conduct on the matter continued unsatisfactory to the last. Three times was he requested to give the names of the new Commissioners,* and three times did he refuse to do so; but, on a threat to stop the progress of the measure, he surrendered, and did as he was asked.

* By Mr. Mundella, July 21st, 1874; and by Mr. W. E. Forster, July 27th and July 28th, 1874.

The Licensing Amendment Act, another reactionary measure of 1874, has been described, and though not so retrograde as the Government had at first designed, was sufficiently so to cause apprehensions as to their future backward steps, and these were far from allayed by the next that was taken. When expounding his first Army Estimates, Mr. Gathorne Hardy had intimated that, though the abolition of purchase in the army was an accomplished fact, he was by no means enamoured with the change of system, and had significantly hinted that something should be done towards the relief of those officers who felt themselves aggrieved by its operation. The hint was fulfilled in a Bill introduced by him in 1875, and designed, according to the exposition of its framer, to facilitate regimental exchanges. It was held by the Opposition that the measure would restore purchase under another name, thus creating an inequality founded on money alone. The Bill, however, was passed without amendment, every attempt at compromise being resisted by the Government, and, of course, rejected by the majority; but clear warning was given that the question would not be settled by the passing of the measure, and that with a Liberal Government the matter would be reopened.

Lord Sandon's Education Bill of 1876, the next retrograde scheme on the list, professed neither to aim at a general reconstruction of our educational system, nor at a reversal of the policy of 1870, and the provisions of the measure as originally stated were not particularly objectionable. The question of direct as against indirect compulsion was the one which was most eagerly fought at first in Committee, and though the religious difficulty soon appeared, the debates were not of the warmth usually characterising education discussions until Mr. Pell introduced an amendment, which was accepted by the Government, proposing to dissolve all School Boards which possessed neither schools nor sites. This attempt at undermining the authority of the new Boards was earnestly protested against by the Liberals, but for three or four sittings without effect. At length, after the Prime Minister had refused to make any concession, Viscount Sandon became somewhat more placable, and the Government were induced to allow that two-thirds of the ratepayers must agree to the dissolution of the Boards. The modifications introduced after the second reading had been so great that Lord Hartington felt it incumbent upon him to move a resolution in disapproval of such vital changes after the principle of the measure had been affirmed; but, even after this, grounds of contention were found, their principal originator being Lord Robert Montagu, who practically proposed that the "25th clause" should be made compulsory. Lord Sandon declined to support this, but was thrown over by the Chancellor of the Exchequer, who accepted it. Another storm ensued, and had not the Government retreated from the reactionary position they had so suddenly taken up, the Opposition would have strained every nerve to defeat the Bill,—a work not supremely difficult at a late period of the session.

But this was not the only storm of 1876. The Queen's Speech of that year informed Parliament and the people that a formal addition was wished to be made to the style and titles of the Sovereign as affecting India, and for this purpose Mr. Disraeli brought a Bill before the House In doing so, he declared that the Princes of India had by various modes conveyed to the Government their desire that such a policy should be pursued; this being but a flight of that active imagination that has stood the Premier in such good stead as a writer of fiction. Before the debate on the second reading, Mr. Disraeli, in reply to Mr. Bright, observed that to state beforehand what title the Queen would take would be binding her down, and not enabling her to exercise her prerogative. Mr. Samuelson put a similar question some days later, and Mr. Disraeli having returned a similar reply, the former gave notice that he would move that the House should not be asked to read the Bill a second time until the proposed addition had been stated. But Mr. Disraeli obviated the necessity for this division by making the required communication in the debate on the second reading, again declaring that native opinion in India favoured its adoption. On the motion to go into Committee, the Marquis of Hartington proposed a resolution directed against the particular title of Empress, and was defeated by a sweeping majority; but before the Bill passed through Committee, Mr. Disraeli pledged himself that "under no circumstances would Her Majesty assume, by the advice of Her Ministers, the title of 'Empress' in England." The third reading was carried by a smaller majority than had previously endorsed the measure, and in the Upper House as many as 91 peers divided against the title of Empress, only 137 voting in its favour. Upon the publication of the proclamation it was found that the Ministry had broken a pledge given in both Houses. They had promised that, instead of inserting limitations in the Bill, the proclamation itself should convey the statement that the title of Empress should be used in India alone; but when the proclamation was issued, it was discovered that no such limitation appeared. The Opposition brought the matter before the House of Commons, which, of course, did Mr. Disraeli's behest to "vindicate the honour of the Government," and the Delhi gathering was the next feature in the scheme.

The measure which has since appeared the most reactionary was the Contagious Diseases (Animals) Act of last year, sometimes called the Dear Meat Bill, as being a title more appropriate to its tendencies. It was avowedly brought in on behalf of the counties against the towns, and the division lists showed that even party ties were broken in order to favour either the producer or the consumer. It is too early to say whether the Bill will have all the effect in elevating prices wished by the farmers, but the suspicion will remain that it was rather the protection of their pockets from foreign competitors than their beasts from foreign diseases that made agriculturists admire the Bill.

"*Startling*" *Successes.*

In such a desert of abortive, permissive, and

reactionary legislation, the oasis of a slight success is startling, and one is inclined to give credit for it to the Ministry, though knowing that some of the measures of which it now assumes to be proud, were either wrung from it, or provided to its hands by political opponents. Among the enactments of its first session for which praise might be claimed are the Rating Bill of Mr. Sclater-Booth, and the Factory Bill of Mr. Cross, the former being substantially that introduced by Mr. Stansfeld in the previous session, and the latter that framed by Mr. Mundella.

The Merchant Shipping Bill of 1875 will be chiefly remembered for the manner in which one man of earnestness, and he an opponent, wrested from the Government a measure they did not care to pass. General satisfaction had been felt when Sir Charles Adderley (now Lord Norton) introduced a Bill dealing with merchant shipping, and some progress had been made with it in Committee, when Mr. Disraeli suddenly announced that in order to pass the Agricultural Holdings Bill (the worthlessness of which has been shown), the Merchant Shipping Bill would not be proceeded with. Then ensued a scene which startled the oldest frequenters of the House. Mr. Plimsoll denounced the "ship-knackers" in no measured terms, and vehemently appealed to the Prime Minister not to send thousands of men to certain death by withdrawing the Bill. The outburst had its effect; alarmed at the emphatic endorsement given by the country to Mr. Plimsoll's appeal, the Government partly drew back from the position they had occupied, and a temporary Bill was run through, giving to the Board of Trade for a year extraordinary powers of detaining ships. The Bill of 1876, introduced in deference to the strong feeling Mr. Plimsoll had aroused upon its predecessor, was very little more satisfactory than that measure of misfortune to the Ministry. But the House would not tolerate it in its original state, and Mr. Plimsoll had the satisfaction of compelling the Government to agree that deck-loading on timber ships should not exceed certain limits.

Three Acts of the session of 1875 furnish the modified successes of which Conservatism is proud. The Home Secretary's Bills for Amending the Labour Laws received valuable help from the Liberal side in their progress through the Commons, and may fairly be considered enactments of the whole House, and not of the dominant majority; whilst Sir Stafford Northcote's Friendly Societies Act was, as the *Times* then said, " modest, if not timid in its provisions." It was, of course, permissive, as has previously been stated. In the next year was passed the Winter Assize Act, which was designed to enable the assizes for several adjoining counties to be held at one place, to be selected for its convenience. This measure, though excellent in its intention, has provided for some parts of the country at least one annual assize more than is required, and has entailed much expense on those living in grouped counties, who have had to leave their own district and go some considerable distance to give evidence. The Commons Act of 1876 was a step in advance of some previous enactments on this matter, but contained an element of danger in allowing discretionary power to remain with the Inclosure Commissioners, who had, it was stated in the course of the debates, during the previous twenty years permitted the appropriation of 400,000 acres, and had only allotted about 4,000 acres for public use, and as compensation for rights surrendered. But the Vivisection Act, allowing physiological experiments upon warm-blooded animals to be performed only by licensed individuals, and the Wild Fowl Preservation Act, prohibiting the killing of sea-fowl between February 15th and July 10th, may fairly be quoted among Government successes.

In 1877, the Prisons Bill, which had had to be withdrawn in the previous Session, was re-introduced, and this time passed. Its object was to provide, as far as possible, for the uniform treatment of prisoners in the different gaols of the country—which it has done by insisting upon the use of the "plank bed"—and to secure a due regard to economy in the management of the prisons—which regard has been somewhat negatived by the manner in which various gaols have been shut, and heavy additional charges entailed upon the rates by boroughs having to send their petty culprits long distances, instead of to the houses of detention they already possessed. When to this measure is added the Irish Intermediate Education Act of 1878, the list of successes will be exhausted. The last named Bill was introduced as a preventive against obstruction, and, being practically unopposed, passed with but little trouble. And this peculiarity is to be noticed with the main measures for which the Government claims credit—that they have been supported by both sides. Those which have been stamped with Liberal opposition have either been withdrawn or have proved failures.

Administrative Fiascoes.

"Empires are now governed like parishes, and a great statesman is only a select vestryman."—Mr. Disraeli *in "Tancred."*

But a dismal record of legislative failure might under certain circumstances be condoned. A Ministry existing on sufferance, or engaged in combat with a strong Power, might be forgiven for not devoting its energies to domestic reform. Neither of these excuses can be urged in favour of the present Government, and even if it could it would not blot from the national memory that which does not so much meet reproach as merit ridicule—the inability to understand the temper of Parliament and the people, and the consequent proposal and subsequent withdrawal of projects deeply offensive to both.

Proposals Withdrawn.

Previous to the indignation caused by the manner in which the Bulgarian Atrocities were treated by the Government, nothing had called forth a deeper feeling during the existence of the Ministry than the issue of the Slave Circulars. The first of these, which was sent out just as Parliament was rising in 1875, instructed naval officers that should a slave escaping from his owner reach a British ship or boat on the high seas, he was to be retained on board. "But," added the Lords of the Admiralty, "when the vessel returns within the territorial limits of the country from a vessel of which the slave has escaped, he will be liable to be surrendered on demand being made, supported by necessary proofs." An outburst of popular feeling followed this sacrifice of anti-slavery principles, and early in October the circular was suspended, and a month later withdrawn. In December another was issued declaring that when a fugitive had been "taken under the protection of the British flag upon the high seas beyond the limit of territorial waters," he was to be retained, if he wished, until he had been landed or transferred "where his liberty will be recognised and respected." With this, however, was coupled the warning that "Her Majesty's ships are not intended for the reception of persons other than their officers and crew;" and the practical result of the whole was that the commander of a ship which might happen to be moored in a harbour where slavery was legally recognised, was forbidden to give shelter to a fugitive slave "unless his life would be in manifest danger if he were not received on board;" and was also ordered "not to entertain any demand for the surrender" of a fugitive slave, nor to "enter into any examination as to his status," but simply to put him ashore within the reach of his masters, and to ask no questions whatever. The popular indignation was not allayed by such alterations, and Mr. Disraeli, in the debate upon the Address in February, 1876, thought it necessary to give a very novel and strikingly commercial reason for the issue of the instructions. He declared that "our officers on foreign stations found themselves every now and then committing acts in the most innocent-minded manner, which ended in actions being brought against them, damages being incurred, and compensation being paid by this country for them." Upon this statement, Mr. J. Holms moved for a return of these actions, from which it appeared that Mr. Disraeli's assertions belonged to the realm of fancy, there having been none brought. Immediately afterwards, Mr. Whitbread proposed to cancel every instruction which might stand in the way of entire protection to fugitive slaves afforded by the British flag, and was met by a proposition to refer the matter to a Royal Commission. After two nights' debate, the latter was carried by 293 to 248, a majority of 45, the smallest the Government has had on any great party question during the existence of the present Parliament, and the number of the minority being the largest (except on Mr. Osborne Morgan's Burials resolution, when it was similar) of any obtained by the Opposition since 1874. The report of the Royal Commissioners laid down that "the officer should be guided before all things by considerations of humanity. Whenever, in his judgment, humanity requires that the slave should be retained on board—as in cases where the slave has been, or is in danger of being, cruelly used—the officer should retain him." Thus humanity, which did not enter into the Prime Minister's calculations, was defined as the basis on which the question should be settled, and the Liberals could claim this as the final victory.

But a proposal equally repugnant to the feelings of the people, though much more speedily acknowledged to be a failure, was that concerning the Rhodope Grant in December last. At that time, with every prospect of an unusually severe winter and of an unparalleled amount of distress, the Government had not thought the suffering of the country worthy of mention in the Queen's Speech. Sir Michael Hicks-Beach had just previously hazarded the opinion that the amount of distress had been much exaggerated for party purposes,—an opinion that was scarcely borne out by the Prime Minister's admission, in the debate on the Address, that the distress was "very great." But it would almost seem as if the Colonial Secretary's belief must also have been that of the Cabinet, for they had no provision to make for the unusual destitution. And this was the ground on which Lord Beaconsfield justified the omission of all reference to it in the Speech from the Throne: "It is a very questionable course," he said, "to allude publicly to the distress of the country when it is not peculiar to the country itself—when you are not yourselves prepared with any remedial measures." Seeing, then, that the Government had no intention of relieving the distress in our own country, it was with a shock of something more than surprise that, a week later, the Commons heard Sir Stafford Northcote give notice of his intention, "on the earliest possible day, to make a motion for a grant in aid of the sufferers in the Rhodope district." The coolness with which the Ministerial benches received the notification was not changed into warmth, even on the challenge of Mr. Anderson that he would move an amendment to the effect "that it is inexpedient, considering the distress which now prevails in the country, that the money of the taxpayers should be devoted to the relief of the district of the Rhodope." The notice of motion was given on a Friday, and before the following Monday the Chancellor of the Exchequer saw the necessity of changing his plans in order to avoid defeat. Accordingly on that day he remarked that the notice had certainly produced a response which, though it had not been given in any formal manner, was sufficient to show that there would be very considerable difference of opinion on the subject, and therefore it was not his intention to proceed with the motion. A short discussion followed, in the course of which Sir Stafford was rather pointedly asked whether the motion was really withdrawn; to which he replied that it had never been made, and that there was no intention of making it. When they made the proposal, he added, they found there could be no doubt that there was a very widely-spread feeling that it was not desirable that such a proposal should be made and discussed. There was a laugh at this point, which appeared somewhat to nettle the Chancellor, who proceeded: "It is all very well to raise a laugh, but we must look at these matters with the eye of common sense; and everybody must see that even if a Government should, at the risk of incurring ridicule, not make a proposal that would lead to repeated debates, and which, if it were adopted, would only be adopted by a majority, it is better that they should not persevere with a proposal which ought not to be accepted in a grudging spirit. I am quite prepared to take my share of any blame that may be cast on us for the manner in which we have acted, and I accept a considerable personal responsibility." The proposition being withdrawn, there was nothing more to be done except to remember that a Government which would make no effort to relieve starvation in England, was fully prepared to tax the already distressed in order to relieve starvation in Turkey.

To the foregoing must be added two matters which have come under the attention of the House during the present session. In the Recess it was freely rumoured that the Government were about to attempt success in a region where Mr. Gladstone had failed—that of Irish University Education. The Irish Chief Secretary and the Romanist Hierarchy were reported to be in constant conclave, all preparations were being matured for a new Conservative aid to the Catholic cause, when, just before Parliament met, it became evident that the negotiations had fallen through. Whether this was through the exorbitant demands of the Irish Catholics, or the energetic threats of the Irish Protestants, is not yet sufficiently apparent; but the soreness that this failure has left behind it has been more than once shown, and the Government's action on the O'Conor Don's Bill has not tended to remove it. Fortunately for appearances, the Ministry in this case found out their danger previous to coming before Parliament with a scheme, but in the matter of the proposed loan of ten millions to India they had not the same good fortune. On March 27th of this year, Mr. E. Stanhope moved for leave to bring in a Bill authorizing the raising of a loan in this country of ten millions for the service of India, the amount of which was not to be added to the permanent debt, but to be met in future years out of the Famine Insurance Fund. Strong hostility was speedily developed, and the recent publication of the order of the Viceroy stopping all public works in order to economise, and indicating that the Famine Insurance Fund was heavily in arrears, has probably given the death-blow to a scheme which was never very lively.

Jobs Accomplished.

The Ministry's sins of commission, in the shape of job appointments, deserve even more reprobation than their sins of omission, in the shape of proposals withdrawn. In more than one case has it happened that persons have been put into places for which they had never shown capacity, because they had been politically or socially useful. To the first of the prominent instances of this mode of dealing with the public service, the notice of Parliament was drawn on July 9th, 1875, when Mr. Dillwyn called attention to the appointment of Sir Alfred Slade, the defeated Conservative candidate for Taunton, as Receiver General of Inland Revenue, he having been put over the heads of all the clerks of the department, including the chief clerk, who had worked through all the grades, and had discharged the duties of the office whilst the previous holder had been incapacitated. The Chancellor of the Exchequer (Mr. Disraeli, with whom the appointment rested, having left the House), replied that as to the selection of Sir Alfred Slade, he "really had nothing particular to say." He thought it was a very hard thing that gentlemen who had entered in the lower ranks should find that the superior Staff appointments were filled unexpectedly by gentlemen outside of the office; but, no doubt, the Receiver Generalship of the Customs and the Receiver Generalship of the

Inland Revenue had generally been regarded as being on a different footing, and were generally given to persons of independent fortune. And there the matter dropped.

In other cases, the subject has not been allowed to pass away so quietly. Notoriously is this so with Lord Hampton, who, as Sir John Pakington, had done yeoman service for the Conservatives for many years. Losing his seat for Droitwich at the Dissolution of 1874, Sir John was made a peer, and, on the death of Sir Edward Ryan in 1875, was appointed Chief Civil Service Commissioner, though then seventy-six years of age. Not only was the salary of £1500 increased to £2000, but an extra commissionership was created at a salary of £1200 to get through the work; and, very naturally, Parliament was asked whether it agreed with the perpetration of such an obvious job. In Committee on the Civil Service Estimates in 1876, it was moved that the additional salary to Lord Hampton and that of a new commissioner should be rejected, but this was defeated by a majority of 25; a proposition, however, to reduce Lord Hampton's salary to the original £1500 was rejected by only 16. On the Report another and much heavier division was taken with the same result, 126 voting against the appointment; and though divisions in 1878 and 1879 have similarly failed to shake Lord Hampton from his post, the smallness of the majorities—10 and 16 respectively—and the increasingly evident difficulty the Ministers feel in defending the appointment, give every hope that the lesson not to perpetrate jobs and create sinecures will be taken to heart. It may be remarked that one of the main grounds the Government assigned for the choice was that it was desirable to have some one in Parliament who would be able to account for the action of the Commissioners. Between his appointment and the end of last session Lord Hampton had addressed the Peers on nine occasions, and not once on any subject connected with his office. In 1876 his topics were Elementary Education (twice), Merchant Shipping, the Sugar Convention, and the Traffic at Hyde Park Corner; in 1877, Coolie Emigration to India; and in 1878, Competitions for the Army (twice), and the Poor Law Amendment Act. This session his name has appeared in a connection of some kind with cathedrals, but, as far as the Civil Service Commission is concerned, he never opens his mouth.

The appointment of Sir Seymour Fitzgerald

about the same time was an open reward for political service. Finding his health fail him, Sir Seymour was about to resign his seat for Horsham, when the Government gave him the post of Chief Charity Commissioner, for which he was admitted to have only a technical qualification. Mr. Disraeli defended the appointment of Sir Seymour on the ground that "it was chiefly by his great exertions and zeal that the Abyssinian Expedition was so successful." * This would have been somewhat of a paradoxical ground even if true, which it happened not to be according to Mr. Disraeli's own showing in July, 1868, when proposing the vote of thanks to the Abyssinian forces.† This was not, however, pointed out at the time, and Sir Seymour's appointment was sanctioned on a division.

The Pigott appointment of 1877 is next on the list, and is chiefly noteworthy as having caused the House of Commons to pass a vote of censure

---

* February 25th, 1876.

† "If we turn from the conduct of the Expedition to the character of the person who commanded it [Sir Robert Napier, now Lórd Napier of Magdala], I think it must be acknowledged that rarely has an Expedition been planned with more providence and executed with more precision. In connection with it everything seems to have been foreseen and everything supplied. It would be presumptuous in me to dwell on the military qualities of the Commander; but all must recognise, and all may admire, the

on Lord Beaconsfield,* which, though subsequently rescinded, was an expression of opinion not lightly to put aside. In this case the Controllership of the Stationery Office, contrary to the recommendations of a Select Committee on the subject, was given to a gentleman inexperienced in the duties, to the exclusion of those better fitted for the post; and the explanation of the Premier rather went to prove the general principle that those are the best chiefs of a department who know the least of its details, than the particular one that Mr. Pigott was the best appointment that could be made.

But though the fact that the father of Mr. Pigott was once vicar of Hughenden may have had nothing to do with his selection, few will be found to doubt that the possession of the Duke of Wellington as uncle, Lord Cowley as father, and Lord Augustus Loftus as father-in-law, will account for that extraordinary promotion of Colonel

sagacity and the patience, the temper and the resource, invariably exhibited" (July 2nd, 1868). The only other officer mentioned by Mr. Disraeli as deserving to be credited with the success of the Expedition was Commodore Heath, who commanded the naval force; and though four others were named in the formal resolution of thanks, among them is not to be found Sir Seymour Fitzgerald, "chiefly by whose great exertions and zeal the Abyssinian Expedition was so successful."

* July 16th, 1877.

Wellesley which has frequently been before the House. This gentleman, in 1871, at twenty-six years of age, was selected to fill the post of Military Attaché at St. Petersburg, for which he received his diplomatic as well as his regimental pay, and his promotion also went on. In 1875, he was made a lieutenant-colonel without purchase, being promoted over the heads of 900 majors, he never having done any duty with his regiment for over four years; and in 1878, being then thirty-three years of age, and not having done a single day's duty with his regiment in the Guards for seven years, and having drawn pay for both his appointments, was made full colonel to the exclusion of 300 lieutenant-colonels and of 1200 field officers in the army, many of whom were in active service when Colonel Wellesley was a mere child. But the appointment of which particular complaint was made was that of Secretary to the Embassy at Vienna, which carried with it a salary of £1000 per annum, and which he obtained over the heads of 90 servants of the Crown whose claims were superior. All these facts were stated in the House of Commons,* and not seriously combated, but Colonel Stanley defended the appointment, though admitting it to be undoubtedly somewhat out of

* May 17th, 1878.

the usual course. And this case also received the sanction of the House.

But to come from outsiders to members of the Administration, what has Sir James Dalrymple Horn Elphinstone, Baronet, and Member for Portsmouth, done to deserve his Lordship of the Treasury? In the session of 1874 he addressed the House on one occasion, and then to explain how it was that the harbour at Galle had been abandoned. Grown bolder by experience, he raised his voice three times during 1875, but never on a subject specially connected with the Treasury, one of his efforts being devoted to talking out a Bill for doing away with church rates in Scotland, because such measures had better be left in the hands of the Government; another to opposing a measure for the abolition of Hypothec in Scotland, because he was an Aberdeenshire proprietor; and the third to speaking against a Bill reforming the Game Laws in the same country, because it was beyond even the power of the House of Commons to turn birds into beasts. In the next year he transferred his oratory to the sister isle, at one time recommending to the consideration of Irish gentlemen interested in fisheries the fact that the piers of Anstruther harbour were constructed of concrete—an observation of which the Speaker remarked that he failed to see the relevancy—and at another—pointedly appealed to by the late Sir Colman O'Loghlen as "one of Her Majesty's Ministers sitting on the front Government bench"—expressing a hope that the Conservative candidate might succeed at a pending election at Longford. It is, perhaps, to the candour of the last remark that the House owes it that, during 1877 and 1878, the two most important sessions of the Parliament, Sir James did not once speak, but he may yet burst forth for the seventh time in six sessions.

There is another member of the Ministry to whom attention may fairly be called, in the shape of Mr. George Augustus Frederick Cavendish Bentinck, the representative of Whitehaven. When Lord Beaconsfield became Premier, he lighted upon Mr. Bentinck as a likely Secretary of the Board of Trade. As an occupant of such a subordinate post is not expected to say much, there is not great fault to be found with Mr. Bentinck for restricting himself in 1874 to suggestions that "we had endless absurdities in the present system of lights" (at sea), and to remarking that some London tramways had been approved of by the local authorities; and in 1875 to making a scattered observation or two on merchant shipping and the registration of trade marks. But when, on Mr. Stephen Cave being engaged by the Khedive, Mr. Bentinck was appointed Judge Advocate-General, he might have been expected to have addressed the House on more than three occasions in 1876, seven in 1877, and three in 1878, some of these only requiring the briefest space in the longest report. That Mr. Stephen Cave, whilst holding the office Mr. Bentinck now fills, was about four times as oratorically active, may not prove that he worked harder, but will at least indicate that he showed more for his money; and when it is remembered what an outcry was raised when Mr. Ayrton was appointed to the offices of Paymaster-General and Judge Advocate-General, it will seem surprising that so little has been heard of the fact that when Mr. Stephen Cave, who succeeded Mr. Ayrton, went to Egypt, not only did he retain his Paymaster-Generalship, but Mr. Cavendish Bentinck was given the post of Judge Advocate-General, two men being thus taken to do the work of one, and so it remains.

But while the Government has been ready to give the taxpayers' money to titled incompetence and aristocratic insufficiency, it has taken opportunity to wring what it could from the strugglers for bread. The manner in which the Reserves were treated last year will be long remembered by those unfortunate men, who, called out in a panic, returned to situations filled and homes broken up, without chance of relief or redress. The case of the reductions at the Army Clothing Department is at the present time arousing public feeling, and will continue to do so until the Ministry display more feeling for the poor. At this establishment, where soldiers' widows are largely employed, and where the average earnings are about 14$s.$ per week, reductions have been effected, varying from 10 to 33 per cent., and averaging 20 per cent., bringing down the 14$s.$ to 11$s.$ 2$\frac{1}{2}d.$ That the Government have acted, to say the least, from inconsiderateness, will appear from the official explanation, as given by Lord [Eustace Cecil:[*] "Factory workers were discharged, while the factory was closed for stock-taking, cleaning, overhauling machinery, etc., to prevent their claiming wages for the period; prices of female labour, piece-work, have been re-arranged, and in some instances reduced." What private firm, wishing to preserve a character for humanity, would dismiss its hands during stock-taking, and

---

[*] April 21st, 1879.

volunteer the statement that this was done "to prevent their claiming wages for the period"?

But the whole course of the Government has been the same—to reward the rich, to reduce the poor; to promote the strong, to punish the weak. Proof of the former has been given; proof of the latter is to be found in the Ministerial attitude upon the *Vanguard* and *Mistletoe* disasters. In the matter of the *Vanguard*, permitting a court-martial to be held upon the officers of that vessel, and refusing to allow one on those of the *Iron Duke*, which ran her down, the Admiralty peremptorily rejected such parts of the verdict of the court-martial as it did not like, fastened the whole responsibility of the disaster on the captain and officers of the *Vanguard*, together with Lieutenant Evans of the *Iron Duke*, dismissed Lieutenant Evans without allowing him the customary right of making a formal defence under legal advice, and acquitted Vice-Admiral Tarleton and Captain Hickley on its own responsibility, and in direct contradiction to the opinions expressed by a court-martial of great experience and authority. In the other case, the Admiralty, in *ex parte* fashion, threw all the blame of the *Alberta's* fatal collision with the *Mistletoe* upon Captain Welch, exonerating Prince Leiningen, the actual captain, from complicity, though declining to hold a court-martial upon these officers, where evidence could have been fairly taken, and each could have offered his defence.

And the Home Office has shown similar specimens of favouritism to those of the War Department and the Admiralty, of which the release of Theodorodi is the most flagrant, it being intensified by comparison with the case of Galley, the difference being that the Sultan pleaded for one, and only the Lord Chief Justice of England for the other. Constantine Theodorodi was sentenced in September, 1877, with a companion, named Paulo Gorlero, to seven years' penal servitude for conspiring to extort money by threats from a lady under circumstances forming, as Mr. Newton, the committing magistrate, said, "one of the most wicked cases he had ever heard of." Last year, at the intercession of the Turkish Ambassador, Theodorodi was secretly liberated, whilst an application by the Italian Ambassador for the release of Gorlero, equally guilty or equally deserving, was rejected, and had not the attention of Parliament been drawn to the matter, this miscarriage of justice would never have been known. In the Galley case, a man was convicted forty years ago of a murder of which, though sent into transportation, he was proved to be innocent. The Lord Chief Justice has furnished Mr. Cross with the most incontestable evidence of this, offering not only himself but a member of the Judicial Committee of the Privy Council as witnesses to its truth, and all he asks for is that, after this lapse of time and with this striking proof, a pardon be granted to the wretched sufferer, who still lives. But Sir Alexander Cockburn is treated with contempt and Musurus Pasha with kindness; the one suppliant, an Englishman, has for over forty years been paying the penalty of a crime he never committed; the other, a Greek favourite of the Sultan, only served a seventh of his time for "one of the most wicked cases ever heard of;" and even-handed justice is still among the things of which Mr. Cross affects to be proud.

If it be asked why so little has been heard of such infractions of the most elementary principles of justice, the answer may be found in words used by Mr. Disraeli twenty-one years ago: "They have in a great degree corrupted the once pure and independent press of England; . . . leading organs are now place-hunters of the cabal, and the once stern guardians of popular rights simper

in the enervating atmosphere of gilded saloons."*
The names of two prominent London organs, distinguished above the others for Ministerial adulation, rise instantly to the thoughts as the most glaring instances of purchased support. One of these has brought the art of political tergiversation to a pitch unrivalled in journalistic history, and, without alteration in proprietorship, averages a change of politics with every new Ministry; the other, having had less opportunity, endeavours to compensate by biting the hand it used to beslaver, and by covering with the coarsest flattery the statesman whom previously it bespattered with the rankest abuse. Not having the power to apply to England what they have shown their will to apply to India—a measure for gagging the expression of independent opinion—the Ministry have suborned those whose proprietors can be bought by exclusive information or a promised peerage; and " it is too true," again to quote the present Premier, " that the shepherds who were once the guardians of the flock, are now in league with the wolves." It is to the credit of the provincial Press that it is only of the London organs that this can be said; but it cannot be too widely known by what means the Government is

* *Speech at Slough*, May 26th, 1858.

ready to purchase support, and by what means some of the tempted have fallen.

Duties Evaded.

How it has happened that such a strong Ministry has so often displayed such an evident weakness may puzzle the historian who does not know the calibre of its members as well as the observers of to-day. The manner in which the Government allowed Sir Daniel Lange to be treated is worth examination if only as showing how an appearance of firmness often hides an actual cowardice. In 1871, Sir Daniel Lange, in private and confidential letters, suggested to Earl Granville, the then Foreign Minister, the purchase of the Suez Canal. By some blunder these communications were published in the Appendix to the Suez Canal papers issued by Mr. Disraeli's Government, and on seeing them M. Charles de Lesseps dismissed Sir Daniel from the post of representative of the Company in this country. Mr. Gladstone drew the attention of the House of Commons to the matter, and suggested that it would be a good test of the great influence we were supposed to have gained in the administration of the Canal if we procured Sir D. Lange's reinstatement; and all the reply Mr. Disraeli practically gave was that he was induced to think that Mr. Gladstone had been unnecessarily alarmed. The mode of dealing with this matter was on a level with that since adopted in the two widely differing cases of Chefket Pasha and Mr. Ogle. In the one a Turkish miscreant, known to have been deeply implicated in the Bulgarian massacres, has not only been allowed to go free but to hold high office under the Porte * despite our remonstrances; in the other an English correspondent's murder by Turkish irregulars has been suffered to go unpunished because it might offend the Sultan to force him to hang a few of his troops. Has the influence of England sunk so low that even Turkey has no fear of it?

Coming from the smaller things to the greater, from the duties evaded in comparatively minor matters to those evaded in important affairs of State, the action of the Ministry towards Greece stands prominently forth. Here was a country which for centuries had groaned under the cruelty of Turkish oppression, and a portion—and a portion only—of which had been liberated, partly through the action of the England of fifty years since. Acting as all nations would in similar

* He is now in a command at Monastir without objection from the English Government; see answer of Mr. Bourke in the House of Commons, April 3rd, 1879.

circumstances, it wished to take advantage of the re-arrangement of the Turkish Empire to have its own again, and was prepared even to use the sword in the effort, when the English Government, by hints of help and promises of consideration, held it back until too late. In his despatch of June 8th, 1878, Lord Salisbury led the Greeks to hope that the English plenipotentiaries at the Congress would do them justice; and after the Berlin gathering was over, Lord Beaconsfield said, at the Knightsbridge dinner, that owing to the exertions of England, "under the Treaty of Berlin, Greece had the opportunity of obtaining a greater increase of territory than would be attained by any of the rebellious provinces;" adding that "the proposition of Lord Salisbury for the rectification of the frontier of Greece really includes all that moderate and sensible men could desire; and that was the plan which was ultimately adopted by the Congress, and which Greece might avail herself of if there was prudence and moderation in her councils." From that time to this Greece has waited with a prudence and moderation highly commendable, but scarcely to be expected, and Turkey does not move a finger to fulfil the Berlin Treaty in her behalf. Now that England is once more endeavouring to hinder France and the other Powers from treading the path of justice, it is beginning to be explained by the Ministerialists that it is altogether optional for the Porte to carry out the clauses affecting Greece, and Lord Beaconsfield has drawn back from the assertion that the proposed concessions to the latter were due to the influence of himself and Lord Salisbury. On April 3rd of this year, the Premier said in the House of Lords: "All that was intended by the notice given by the plenipotentiary for France with regard to what should be the materials of a satisfactory settlement, was accepted by the Powers in that spirit; and nearly at the end of the Conference, the President said that no Power was bound by the suggestion which had been made by the French plenipotentiary, and certainly not Turkey." If the Porte was "certainly not" to be bound, who was to be? It was from Turkey that the Greeks were to receive the territory rightly theirs, and it is now Turkey that refuses to do that to which it then agreed. And the Greeks have found, by the bitterness of experience, that the promise of aid from an English Conservative Government, is about as valuable as that of a rectification of frontier from a Turkish Sultan.

The Uncalled-for Undertaken.

The purchase of the Suez Canal shares of the Khedive for £4,080,000, hailed as it was as a transcendent stroke of policy, is now little heard of, for its glory has long since departed. From the platform of the *haute politique,* upon which it was hoisted in November, 1875, Ministers in defending it in the House of Commons in February, 1876, had to bring it down to a financial and commercial consideration, and to strive to show that the bargain was worth the making, the Company being solvent and its business expanding. But it is not yet forgotten that, for their share in the transaction, the Messrs. Rothschild obtained £98,000—a substantial addition to the cost of the shares—besides the facilities for speculating in Egyptian bonds, of which such well-known financiers can scarcely be expected not to have availed themselves.

The Anglo-Turkish Convention, with the acquisition of Cyprus, similarly saluted on first appearance, similarly receives no present reference at Conservative feastings. But, unlike the Suez Canal shares, it cannot be claimed for it that the bargain was worth the making. We have assumed the protectorate of Asia Minor, and the sovereignty of an island " in a dead angle of the Mediterranean," in order to civilize the inhabitants and conquer the Russians. The second we shall not be called upon to do in that part of the world, and the first we shall fail in even if we attempt it, which is doubtful. The Sultan wants that which the English refuse to give; he demands money to reform his provinces, and we decline to send him that which would renovate harems and enrich pashas. As a consequence, Asia Minor is not to be reformed, and Cyprus will not be made " an important place of arms " for much the same reason. In the island fever as well as finance stands in our way, for a climate which prostrates a heavy percentage of our soldiers, and a country which demands a heavy percentage of our revenue, combine, with the imminent possibility of famine, to make Cyprus one of the most troublesome of all the burdens received from the Porte. And as if natural difficulties were not sufficient to make the Ministry repent of its bargain, Sir Garnet Wolseley's *locum tenens* seems to have allowed an outrage upon the religious sensibilities of the Cypriote Christians, by the degradation of the two Greek priests at Famagusta, which must breed future trouble. In all the cases named of things uncalled-for which the Government has undertaken, the haste with which they have been done is a marked feature,—about a week serving in each case to put the country into embarrassments from which years will not free.

Treasury Bench Vacillation.

The firmness which results in the constant accumulation of difficulties abroad, has only been equalled by the vacillation which has similar effects at home. This was first strikingly displayed within a very few months of the General Election. The late Mr. Ward Hunt, in introducing the Navy Estimates in 1874, after severe censures on the "so-called economies" of the Liberal Government, and after insinuating that they had neglected the building of new ships and the repair of the old ones, and that of our forty-one sea-going ironclads only nine were good for anything at all, declared: "As long as I remain at the Admiralty it must be understood that I do not mean to have a fleet on paper; that whatever ships appear as forming a part of the strength of the Navy must be real and effective ships, and not dummies." Mr. Goschen, the ex-First Lord, remarked upon this that, were these things so, the Government ought to propose to remedy matters out of the immense surplus left them by the Gladstone Administration, but Sir Stafford Northcote explained away Mr. Ward Hunt's apprehensions, answering that, as they objected very much to the principle of violent reduction, they equally objected to "any violent launching into sudden expenditure."

But even this was not so striking an illustration of the ease with which the Government explained away or abandoned that which caused them difficulty, as was furnished the next year over the Judicature Bill. In 1874, one of the Government measures had been a Bill of the Lord Chancellor's to complete Lord Selborne's Judicature Act, which was "massacred" in the House of Commons, but again brought into the House of Lords in 1875, and read a second time without a division. But the opposition which was apparently so feeble in point of numbers was all-powerful in point of influence. A caucus was formed, in which Lord Redesdale and the Duke of Buccleuch were prominent, and the manner in which the members of this secret committee worked upon the Government may be gathered from the fact that, without waiting to go into Committee and test the strength of the Opposition forces in the only constitutional manner, the Ministry, with the most lamentable expressions of disappointment on the part of the Lord Chancellor, threw up the Bill without a division, upon which Lord Selborne declared: "That a Bill of this importance should be got rid of in this manner is not, in my opinion, creditable to your Lordships' House, fair to the country, or calculated to do honour to Her Majesty's Government."

In April, 1875, while the proceedings of the Select Committee on Foreign Loans were pending, Mr. C. E. Lewis called the attention of the House to a letter addressed to the Chairman of the Committee, reflecting on Captain Bedford Pim, M.P., which had been published in the *Times* and *Daily News*. Mr. Lewis proposed that the printers of these journals should be directed to attend at the bar for breach of privilege, and though these motions were resisted, they were carried. But on the afternoon when the printers, who had about as much to do with the matter published as the boys who vended their papers, appeared, obedient to the call, Mr. Disraeli, who had acquiesced in the previous proceedings, changed front, and moved that the order commanding their attendance should be read and discharged, which was agreed to, and this latest attempt to intimidate the Press failed for very feebleness.

The manner in which Irish Sunday Closing was first repelled and then assisted is another curiosity of the history of this Parliament. In 1875, on the second reading of the late Mr. R. Smyth's Bill, Sir M. Hicks-Beach opposed it, his impression being that it would tend to create disorder, and that immediate and universal Sunday closing could not be safely or properly carried out.* The measure was "talked out" on that occasion, and the next year,† Sir Michael, on a motion to a similar effect, explicitly denied that he had ever meant to hint that he was prepared to accept the principle of total Sunday closing in town or country, urging that they ought not to agree to it merely because Irish opinion desired it, and that it logically carried with it the principle of the Permissive Bill; venturing further to suggest that an abstract motion, even if successful, could lead to no practical result, at any rate for some time to come. Upon a division the motion was carried by 224 to 167, a majority of 57, Sir Stafford Northcote, Mr. Cross, Mr. Gathorne Hardy, Lord John Manners, Sir C. Adderley, and Viscount Sandon, voting in the minority, which was "told" by the Govern-

* May 5th, 1875.
† May 12th, 1876.

ment whips. Two months later,* Mr. Smyth introduced a Bill based on the resolution; Sir Michael announced that the Government had decided not to oppose it, and it was read a second time without a division. The next year † Sir Michael adhered to this decision, and the consequence of this is that the Bill is now law. Of course it might be argued that in thus submitting to the declared wish of the House of Commons, though against its own convictions, the Ministry acted in praiseworthy fashion. But even if it were a proof of virtue in a Government to accept that which it believed to be wrong merely because it was willed by the majority, the present holders of office could not claim much from it. For on two occasions,‡ the Colonial Marriages Bill has been read a second time in the Lower House by a substantial majority, despite the opposition of the Ministry; and yet every obstacle has been placed in the way of its further progress, though it would secure the loyalty of powerful colonies.

But a stranger habit than that of causing a Minister to eat his own words is that, which

* July 12th, 1876.
† February 12th, 1877.
‡ February 28th, 1877, and February 27th, 1878.

has been somewhat frequent, of putting up one to answer another. This was first displayed in 1874, when Sir Stafford Northcote had to calm the passions aroused by Lord Sandon on the Endowed Schools Bill; and in 1876, when the process was exactly reversed, on the Education Amendment Bill. The mode in which Mr. Disraeli evaded the difficulties of the first-mentioned Bill, by throwing the blame on the draughtsman, has already been told; and the manner in which Sir Stafford Northcote had to explain away Sir Charles Adderley on the Merchant Shipping Bill forms an amusing chapter in political reminiscences. But these were paralleled in every way by the strangeness of conduct displayed on two prominent occasions in 1877. In the one (as has been told) Mr. Sclater-Booth "whipped" the squires against county boards and then deserted them;* and in the other, Mr. E. Stanhope having carefully demolished Mr. J. R. Yorke's contentions in favour of a Royal Commission to inquire into the Stock Exchange, the Chancellor of the Exchequer put him on one side and accepted the motion.† More recent instances of this practice, which does not

* March 9th, 1877.
† March 20th, 1877.

heighten the respect due to Ministers, have not been rare, one being as recent as May 2nd, when Mr. Lowther opposed, and Sir Stafford Northcote accepted, Mr. Shaw-Lefevre's proposition for an inquiry into the working of the Irish Land Act. This session, also, whilst the Government attitude towards the Municipal Qualifications Abolition Bill of Mr. Mundella and the Poor Law Amendment Act Amendment Bill of Mr. T. W. Mellor has been, at the least, ambiguous, towards the Bill for the abolition of Hypothec it has been misleading, an apparent support being given to that much-called-for and previously-opposed measure, and the majority of Ministers in the House going into the lobby against it,—a piece of electioneering tactics not sufficiently clever to deceive even a Midlothian "faggot." And these are only a few instances of the vacillation which characterises the Treasury Bench.

MINISTERIAL FABLES.

"There is no act of treachery or meanness of which a political party is not capable; for in politics there is no honour."—MR. DISRAELI *in "Vivian Grey."*

Even Ministries whose members are talented and majorities sure occasionally meet with failures and embark in fiascoes; but it is seldom indeed that against any English Government the accusation of falsehood can be brought. It is one of the most serious allegations that could be made, and should only be put forward with the strongest proofs. That this Ministry deserves to be so branded must be judged from the statements now to be urged. Upon these rest the charge that the Government has often refrained from telling the whole truth, and that some of its members have more than once told something but the truth.

Contradictions.

"I do feel that there is nothing in this country so important, not in the legal or technical sense, but in the higher view, as that the Government should keep faith with Parliament."—MR. GATHORNE HARDY (*now* VISCOUNT CRANBROOK), *Debate on Sir Robert Collier's appointment*, February 19th, 1872.

There have been so many instances of Ministerial contradiction already given that it may be difficult to avoid repeating some of them; but to the first there has been, as yet, no reference. In his 1874 address to the electors of Greenwich Mr. Gladstone promised the repeal of the Income Tax; and in his to the electors of Bucks the now Lord Beaconsfield virtually volunteered to do the same, stating that the abolition of that tax was a measure which the Conservative party had always favoured. But subsequently it seems to have been felt that this declaration went too far, for speaking at Newport Pagnell Mr. Disraeli explained thus: " When I said in my address to you that the Conservative party favoured the repeal of the Income Tax, I said it, as all of you thoroughly understand, with a due deference, of course, to the circumstances and conditions of things." Yet, although the surplus, instead of the four millions which Mr. Gladstone had promised, was, according to Sir Stafford Northcote's first Budget statement, as nearly as possible, if not actually, six millions, the Income Tax was not repealed. According to the Chancellor of the Exchequer, despite the positive assertions of his chief about two months before, it would have been " wrong and culpable," on so short a notice, to have done so, his proposition being, as " an amount of relief to which the taxpayers are under the circumstances justly entitled," to simply remove a penny from it. But perhaps Mr. Disraeli would have justified this as he did another of his broken pledges. On April 14th, 1874, Lord Robert Montagu asked him whether the *Times* had correctly reported two of his election speeches of the previous February, the gist of which may be gathered from the conclusion of the question: "And whether he now judges that 'laws of coercion and stringent severity that do not exist in any other quarter of the globe' are 'necessary' for the government of Ireland by the British Parliament?" And Mr. Disraeli commenced his reply by saying: "It is some time since the observations referred to by the noble Lord were made, and a good deal has happened in the interval"—the "some time since" being just two months, and the "good deal" the removal of the speaker from Opposition to office.

The flippancy of this answer was equalled by that of the replies Mr. Disraeli gave in the summer of 1876, on the Bulgarian horrors, in which true stories of wholesale massacre were treated as "coffee-house babble,"* the Bulgarians were "sufferers by imaginary atrocities,"* and torture declared to be doubtful "among an Oriental people who generally terminate their connection with culprits in a more expeditious manner."† But this was only excelled by the statement that communications had reached the Government from the Consul at Philippopolis, † where

* July 31st, 1876.
† July 10th, 1876.

there was, as a fact, no such official.* These errors so nearly amount to positive mis-statements, that it is necessary to offer some apology for considering them in a lighter category, but the Premier's memory is so defective that it is only fair to make such allowance. Another instance of this was given in the Aylesbury speech of September, 1876, in which, although Lord Beaconsfield declared that communications on some plan of Lord Derby were "occurring constantly" between the Powers immediately after the destruction of the European concert by England's refusal to accept the Berlin Memorandum, not a trace of any of these can be found in the blue-books presented to Parliament.

The Duke of Richmond's self-contradictory versions of the vital principle of the Government Burials Bill rank with those given by Sir Stafford Northcote of the Pigott appointment, the latter's excuse for his second statement differing from the original, being that on the first occasion he had not made himself acquainted with the facts.* Perhaps it was for this last reason that, while Lord Derby, as Foreign Secretary, declared that "as far as the Government is concerned, we shall not depart from the

* Despatch from Sir H. Elliot.   † July 23rd, 1877.

ordinary custom of sending an ambassador" to the impending Congress,* and proved most conclusively that in a Parliamentary system of Government, the Foreign Secretary could not attend, consistently with his position in the Cabinet, Lords Beaconsfield and Salisbury resolved to go, though the former admitted he could furnish no precedent for such a course.† And equally as much as the Premier was at variance with the late Foreign Secretary on this point, so is he with the present one as to the North-Western frontier of India, Lord Salisbury declaring it to be "very minutely marked out" ‡ and Lord Beaconsfield averring it to be "haphazard." § After these specimens of the most palpable contradictions, the difference between the explanations of the Prime Minister and the Secretary of War ‖ on the Queen's letter to Lord Chelmsford, the one saying it had been sent "on the full responsibility of the Ministry,"

* February 21st, 1878.
† June 3rd, 1878.
‡ June 11th, 1877: "The bounds of that [the Indian] Empire are very minutely marked out, *especially on the North-Western side.* . . . There is no doubt whatever as to what the frontier of British India is. It is perfectly well known."
§ November 9th, 1878: "Our North-Western frontier is a *haphazard*, and not a scientific frontier."
‖ March 18th, 1879:—" That message [of the Queen to Lord

and the other stating that he was alone responsible, surprises no more than the Chancellor of the Exchequer's description of a deliberate statement of Lord Beaconsfield concerning Cyprus as a "figure of speech."*

Equivocations.

"I was told with great severity by the present Secretary of State for Foreign Affairs [the Marquis of Salisbury] speaking in the House of Lords, that 'he who employs a less accurate term when a more accurate one is available is guilty of tampering with the purity of truth.'"—THE RIGHT HON. MONTAGUE BERNARD, *letter to the "Times,"* April 22nd, 1879.

The careful manner in which the leading members of the Ministry have often fenced with facts is no less worthy of notice than the careless way in which they have occasionally contradicted themselves. Mr. Disraeli's statements in the debates on the Endowed Schools and Royal Titles Bills, especially the latter, concerning the supposititious wish of the Indian Princes for the measure, have been already indicated. But what Mr. Disraeli once said of Lord Cranborne's

Chelmsford] was transmitted under the responsibility of her advisers . . . It has been done *on the full responsibility of the Ministry.*" (LORD BEACONSFIELD.)—"I did not think it necessary to consult my colleagues on the matter, and *I am responsible* for having thought it consistent with my duty to transmit that message." (COLONEL STANLEY.)

* March 31st, 1879.

invective may be remarked of these assertions—they "lacked finish," for they could not impose upon anyone. It was different with Batoum, for the manner in which Lord Beaconsfield persuaded his followers, who for months had wanted to rush into war to save it to the Turk, that it was not worth having, was as clever as the further assertion with which he endeavoured to persuade them that Turkey was better off since the war than before it. Unfortunately for the *persiflage* anent Batoum, it was proved by Hobart Pasha, no enemy of a Turcophile Premier, to be untrue *; but nevertheless the treatment of

---

* "But let us see *what is this Batoum of which you have heard so much?* It is generally spoken of in society and in the world as if it were a sort of Portsmouth—whereas, in reality, *it should rather be compared with Cowes. It will hold three considerable ships, and* if it were packed like the London Docks, it *might hold six; but in that case the danger, if the wind blew from the north, would be immense.*"—LORD BEACONSFIELD, *Explanation of Congress Proceedings,* July 18th, 1878.

* "*Batoum* is more than a bay; it *is a harbour, though small, and a very safe one, as no sea or wind ever endangers the safety of ships moored to the shore.* It is well known to sailors that all vessels immediately on entering the harbour have to secure their sterns to the shore, where they are quite safe. *Thirteen men-of-war of different sizes, of which six were ironclads, and two large wooden frigates, were lying moored to the shore on more than one occasion.*"—HOBART PASHA, *letter to Earl Granville, read in the House of Lords,* July 26th, 1878.

Lord Salisbury's "important harbour of Batoum"*
as "a sort of Cowes" † was clever even if not
creditable.

But neither clever nor creditable have been
the attacks of Lord Beaconsfield upon Mr. Gladstone. The insinuation in the Aylesbury Speech
that his predecessor in high office was worse
than Chefket Pasha or Achmet Aga, causes a
smile rather than indignation; and the same may
be said of the Knightsbridge attack ‡ upon "a
sophistical rhetorician, inebriated with the exuberance of his own verbosity, and gifted with an
egotistical imagination that can at all times
command an interminable and inconsistent series
of arguments to malign an opponent and to glorify
himself." But when, in the House of Lords, §
Lord Beaconsfield stated that Mr. Gladstone had

---

* Despatch to the Powers, April 1st, 1878.

† July 18th, 1878.

‡ July 27th, 1878.

§ July 29th, 1878 : "The speaker [Mr. Gladstone] on several occasions took occasion to make personal allusions to me—allusions intended to be very offensive, though I must say that I was undisturbed by them. I may allude to the speech at Oxford, which was not an after-dinner speech, but one made in cold blood, and in which the right hon. gentleman singled me out of the Cabinet, charged me with all the offences of the Cabinet, and described me as a dangerous and even devilish character. . . . It was a long time before I took any notice of criticisms coming from that quarter . . . as, during the more or less excited rhetorical campaign of called him "a dangerous and even devilish character," and had "indulged in criticisms replete with the most offensive epithets" as to his conduct, it might have been expected that he would have attempted to justify his observations when challenged * by the one he attacked. This, however, though immediately and ostentatiously promised, has never been done.† It is small wonder, when a Prime Minister could thus bring himself

---

the previous two years, the right hon. gentleman had indulged in criticisms replete with the most offensive epithets as to my conduct, and in description of my character."

* July 30th, 1878.

† "I requested Lord Beaconsfield to point out where and how I had described him as a devilish character, and what were the offensive epithets applicable to his character with which my speeches abounded. He answered with very great promptitude, and from his answer it appeared that the particular epithet—which I will not again repeat—had never been used at all by me, but had been used, as it appeared, by some gentleman who concurred in my political convictions. With respect to the string of offensive epithets, Lord Beaconsfield stated, most reasonably, that that was a question not to be answered in a moment, but that it required searching, and that a search should be made. I agreed to that most reasonable demand, and I determined that I would not be impatient or particular as to the time to be occupied n this investigation. Well, three months have passed away, and I have not heard one single word on the subject of those offensive epithets of a personal character with which the House of Lords was solemnly assured, from the highest quarter, a series of my speeches had been embellished."—MR. GLADSTONE *at Rhyl*, October 31st, 1878.

to make unfounded allegations against a political opponent, that one of his favourite subordinates, Sir Henry Layard, should follow in his wake, and be defended by his masters.

Lord Cranbrook, who, as Mr. Gathorne Hardy, was a hard but fair hitter, developed a diplomatic talent in the Upper House which had not been suspected of him in the Commons. This was certainly not displayed when, in the hearing of a crowded house, he is stated to have ejaculated "That's a lie!" after a revelation of Lord Derby's;* but it first appeared in the Afghan despatch of November 18th, 1878. In Paragraph 9 of that historical document, he managed to convey the impression that the Governments of Lord Northbrook in India and Mr. Gladstone at home were so at variance in 1873 as to sow the first seeds of the recent struggle. As a beginning this would have been more satisfactory if it had not proved to be baseless,† but the strength of

* July 18th, 1878.

† "I have read with much surprise, and I confess with some indignation, the 9th paragraph of Lord Cranbrook's despatch. It seems to me to be carefully and not unskilfully drawn, so as to suppress the most important facts, and to put a misleading construction upon those which are supplied."—THE DUKE OF ARGYLL, *letter to the* "*Times,*" November 23rd, 1878.

"I think I have shown that the inferences which have been generally drawn from Lord Cranbrook's despatch—namely, that the Treasury Bench in the Lords—which can already boast a Prime Minister, who was point blank contradicted on questions of fact three times in one speech * by the leader of the Opposition, and a Foreign Secretary who can insinuate that a former colleague resembles Titus Oates †—this strength cannot but be increased by an Indian Secretary who can "carefully and not unskilfully draw [a despatch] so as to suppress the most important facts, and to put a misleading construction upon those which are supplied."

One further equivocation may be briefly dismissed. Lord Beaconsfield and his colleagues, when asked to produce papers, make a point of urging delay—either the time is not ripe for their publication, or the printer takes a long time getting them out of hand. The former is often an excuse to prevent discussions not necessarily inconvenient to the country, but certainly so to

when I was Viceroy in 1873 I wished to comply with Shere Ali's request for assurances of protection, but I was overruled by the Home Government, and that there was a change of policy with regard to complying with the request he made in 1873, after Mr. Disraeli succeeded Mr. Gladstone as Prime Minister, are not in accordance with the facts of the case."—LORD NORTHBROOK, *Memorandum on Viscount Cranbrook's Despatch*, November 28th, 1878.

* January 17th, 1878. † July 18th, 1878.

Ministers. The latter may be set down at once as worthless. The resources of any great printing establishment are so great in these days that even the largest blue-book of despatches would be a matter of days and weeks and not of months. When such a one as that containing the Afghan papers was deliberately held back for months on the plea of the printer—a book that a private firm could have got out in a fortnight—it was time to expose a hollow pretence which could only deceive those who knew absolutely nothing about it.

Mis-statements.

"There has been a lying spirit abroad."—MR. CROSS, *Debate on the Vote of Credit*, January 31st, 1878.

Several of the contradictions and equivocations already given would have fairly come under the head " mis-statements " had it not been reserved for those " gross as a mountain, open, palpable," which cannot be explained away. The first of these was made apparent in the debates on the Public Worship Regulation Bill, in which Mr. Disraeli, describing Lord Salisbury, then, as now, his colleague, as " a great master of gibes, and flouts, and jeers," * severely attacked him for

* August 5th, 1874.

having taunted "respectable men like ourselves" as being "a blustering majority." The next night * Lord Salisbury retorted that "the most extraordinary language" had been imputed to him "by persons, or by a person who was evidently wholly unacquainted with the matter of which he was speaking." He did not know who "invented the idea," but it was "a simple and absolute fabrication." All of which looked as if the Ministry were an eminently happy family.

But if anyone were sufficiently unkind to cast back Lord Salisbury's language upon its author, after reading his declaration concerning the Peshawur Conference, it would be difficult to dispute his right to do so. For at a time when the Ameer Shere Ali had been harassed by Lord Lytton's attempts to compel him to accept a Resident, the then Indian Secretary stated in the Lords: † "We have not tried to force an Envoy upon the Ameer at Cabul," and added, "There is no reason for any apprehension of any change of policy or of disturbance in our Indian Empire." ‡ Lord Beaconsfield was equally precise

* August 6th, 1874.
† June 15th, 1877.
‡ "We have heard from the noble Marquis that we need be under no apprehension of any substantial change in the policy pursued towards the Ameer of Afghanistan. . . . We have heard from the

in statement, aided by Lord Salisbury in innuendo, that on January 17th, 1878, there were no dissensions in the Cabinet,* Lord Carnarvon

noble Marquis that it is not correct to say that the Ameer of Afghanistan has been pressed to receive a British Resident at Cabul, or that there was any intention, as I understood the noble Marquis, of sending a British force from India to Afghanistan with any hostile intent. Now, that was the rumour which caused me and others much anxiety ... The policy we have pursued with regard to the Ameer has been to show him that we desired to assist him with our advice whenever he requires it, and not to press upon him the presence of British officers in his territories, unless he really desires that they should go there, and will give him a welcome. ... It is with great satisfaction, therefore, that I have heard the assurance of the noble Marquis that the policy I have referred to Her Majesty's Government will continue to pursue. *I am satisfied that he has given us that assurance in perfect good faith*, and that we may trust him to resist any attempt to put it aside."—LORD NORTHBROOK *in the House of Lords*, June 15th, 1877.

* " The noble Earl [Granville] knows very well that *there is not the slightest evidence that there has ever been any difference between my opinions and those of my colleagues* [the Earls of Derby and Carnarvon] whom he has quoted with approbation and sympathy."—LORD BEACONSFIELD, *Debate on the Address*, January 17th, 1878.

"As to the disunion in the Cabinet, I was anxious to know on what grounds that charge rested, and as far as I could see there were only two—one was that Musurus Pasha had praised the Turkish Constitution, whereas I had condemned it; and the other was our old friends the newspapers."—The MARQUIS OF SALISBURY, *Debate on the Address*, January 17th, 1878.

"The statement that I or my noble friend [the Marquis of Salisbury] ever declared to this House that there had been no difference of opinion in the Cabinet between its various members having resigned two days previously;* and on the same night so misrepresented Earl Granville, as has been stated before, that he was forced three times to correct himself. It was on the same night that the Premier declared "that from the very first there has never been any hesitation by Her Majesty's Government as to the course of policy which they would pursue" in Eastern affairs, the fact being that the order to the Fleet to go into the Dardanelles, issued two or three days previously, had been cancelled,† because of

---

is one *utterly unfounded*. No such statement was ever made."—LORD BEACONSFIELD, *in reply to Earl Granville*, July 29th, 1878.

* "Your Lordships will observe that *three times within three weeks it has been my misfortune to be at material variance* on a matter of the highest importance *with my colleagues;* and that *twice during that interval I have felt myself constrained to place my resignation in the hands of the Prime Minister* on this particular subject."—LORD CARNARVON, *Personal Explanation*, January 25th, 1878.

† "It was then decided [at a Cabinet Council, January 15th, 1878] to move the Fleet into the Dardanelles. My Lords, I entertained the strongest objection to that course, both with reference to the time at which it was proposed to adopt the measure, and to the proceeding itself; and on the following day I wrote to the Prime Minister requesting him to submit my resignation to the Queen as soon as the Fleet should sail. *Meanwhile circumstances seem to have occurred to change his mind, and on the following day* I learned that *the order to the Fleet was cancelled*."—LORD CARNARVON, *Personal Explanation*, January 25th, 1878.

the resignations of Lords Derby and Carnarvon. Better things might have been expected of Sir Stafford Northcote, but he also stooped to deceive the House of Commons on the very day* that preparations were being made in India for the despatch of Native troops to Europe, by saying: "I can assure the House we make this proposal [for an unusually long Easter adjournment] with no concealed designs, or any intentions of a

---

* April 16th, 1878: "*Nothing whatever has occurred which should give occasion for increased anxiety. . . . At this moment there is nothing in our policy at all different from that which we have repeatedly declared to this House.* There is no change in the views which we expressed in the debate which occurred only a week ago. . . . Nothing in the situation has altered for the worse since the time we last had to communicate with Parliament on the subject, and we say with the most perfect confidence that we see no reason whatever to apprehend any inconvenience from the rising of Parliament for the time we have mentioned. . . . *I can assure the House we make this proposal with no concealed designs, or any intentions of a mischievous character;* but we do that which we have declared, weeks and weeks ago, we proposed to do, which is in itself reasonable, and which we have no reason to believe we ought to depart from." Upon this, Mr. W. E. Forster observed, "*I cannot suppose, considering* the proposal to adjourn for three weeks, and also *the satisfactory statement which the Chancellor of the Exchequer made* in the early part of to-day's sitting, *that the Government can for a moment contemplate anything like a war policy during the Recess.*" In the evening papers of the next day (April 17th), and simultaneously with the Chancellor's statement, appeared a Reuter's telegram, dated Calcutta that day, saying: "*The Indian Government has received orders to despatch troops to Malta.*"

mischievous character;" justifying himself afterwards * by asserting that "there was no reason" why such a step should be communicated to Parliament. Lord Salisbury's assurance † that the abstract published by Marvin of the Salisbury-Schouvaloff Agreement was "wholly unauthentic" and, "not deserving of confidence," was on a level with the whole morality of that surreptitious bond; and the Duke of Richmond and Gordon took part of a leaf out of the Foreign Secretary's book when ‡ he described the full draft as incomplete and "consequently" inaccurate. But the Session was not to close without the Premier again exposing his statements to a

---

* May 6th, 1878: "I can only say that *the decision of Her Majesty's Government* to order a certain number of Indian troops to Malta *was one arrived at some time ago; but* that *it was not thought necessary*, nor is it according to practice, *that such a decision should be communicated to Parliament.* . . . I may say that *the Government generally were not prepared for the matter becoming known so soon.* . . . But, *under any circumstances*, I may frankly say that *we should not have thought it our duty* —even if we had not foreseen that the matter would become public in so short a time—*to have made a communication to Parliament with respect to it* until the arrangements had been made. *There was no reason why it should be done*, and we saw much inconvenience in premature discussions and disclosures on the subject."

† June 3rd, 1878.

‡ June 17th, 1878.

flat denial, by taking occasion, in an answer to Earl Granville,* to observe that Lords Derby and Carnarvon "had given their adherence to a policy which when the time came to carry into effect they shrank from the responsibility of so doing." To this Lord Carnarvon took the earliest opportunity † of giving "an absolute and unqualified contradiction." Lord Beaconsfield and Batoum, Lord Salisbury and "Titus Oates," fittingly belonged to a Session in which so many strange statements had been made; and during the Recess, as if determined not to allow the favourite Ministerial weapon to blunt for want of usage, Lord Beaconsfield stated at Guildhall ‡ that "former Viceroys have had their attention called with

* July 29th, 1878: "We adhered to the policy which we understood those two distinguished noblemen [the Earls of Carnarvon and Derby] who resigned had accepted, and which I understood they were prepared to carry into effect. We thought they had given their adherence to *a policy which, when the time came to carry into effect, they shrank from the responsibility of so doing.*"

† August 1st, 1878: "*If the noble Earl means*—I am speaking for myself now—*that I, having agreed to particular measures of policy . . . when the moment arrived shrank from the responsibility which that act and those measures involved,*—then *I must*, with all courtesy, but in the strongest language I can command and Parliamentary usage allows, *give the statement an absolute and unqualified contradiction.*"

‡ November 9th, 1878.

anxiety to the state of our [North-Western] frontier,"—to which Lord Northbrook gave a distinct contradiction.*

It would seem from present indications that the Session of 1879 will in mis-statement somewhat rival that of 1878. Despite the fact that previously on the same evening† Lord Cranbrook

* " The Prime Minister said the other night that 'the attention of Viceroys and of Governments in India and in England has for a long time been directed to the question of the North-Western frontier of our Indian Empire.' It was not, however, considered in my time. My military advisers—Lord Napier of Magdala, and Sir Henry Norman, second to none in knowledge and experience—never brought to the notice of the Government of India that our frontier required rectification, during the four years I passed in India. I have the highest authority for saying that during the Administration of Lord Mayo no such considerations were brought forward; but in the years 1867 and 1868, under Lord Lawrence's Administration, the question was fully considered on more than one occasion. . . . The conclusions of the Government of India at the time were given in these words:—' We object to any interference in the affairs of Afghanistan by a forcible or amicable occupation of any post or tract in this country beyond our own frontier, inasmuch as we think such a measure would, under present circumstances, engender irritation, defiance, and hatred in the minds of Afghans, without in the least strengthening our power either for attack or defence.' "—LORD NORTHBROOK, *Speech at Winchester*, November 11th, 1878.

† March 25th, 1879:—"The noble Marquis [Lansdowne] condemns the Government in that, having censured Sir Bartle Frere for acting with precipitation, for taking responsibility on himself which belonged to the Government alone, they have left him in the position he occupies in South Africa. My Lords, it is one thing

had contended that it was one thing to censure and another to recall Sir Bartle Frere, the Marquis of Salisbury said that the Government had "expressed no opinion upon the policy" of the ex High Commissioner. The answers of Mr. Cross and Mr. Bourke on the release of Theodorodi have been equally contradictory. At first * Mr. Bourke stated that he had been dealt with in the ordinary course; then Mr. Cross said † that it was on an informal application of the Turkish Ambassador, but finally ‡ had to admit that it was a formal application, on behalf, of course, of the Sultan. So that even on minor points Ministers cannot agree either with themselves or each other for a few nights running.

V.—PERSONAL GOVERNMENT AND IMPERIALISM.

"Depend upon it the English people love not the exercise of arbitrary power."—MR. CROSS, *Debate on Sir Robert Collier's appointment*, February 19th, 1872.

It would, perhaps, be somewhat difficult, even to censure; it is another thing to recall." (VISCOUNT CRANBROOK.) "They [the Government] have expressed no opinion upon the policy of Sir Bartle Frere. . . . Noble lords opposite have too readily assumed that we have censured the conduct or policy of Sir Bartle Frere." (THE MARQUIS OF SALISBURY.)

* March 7th, 1879.   † March 11th, 1879.   ‡ March 28th, 1879.

for the members of the Ministry, to define the "Imperialism" so lately and so loudly preached. If it merely means the protection of the best interests of the Empire, every Englishman is an Imperialist. But if it means the spread of annexation and the growth of absolutism, a loss to liberty and a gain to power, every Englishman who loves his country will be earnest in his protest against it. The nation has grown too wise to rest its faith in military glory or despotic kings, but it must watch lest its freedom be encroached upon by the specious pretexts of the flatterers of the Court.

The tendency of Ministerial policy, whatever its design, has been to exalt the Crown at the expense of Parliament. The mystery with which the most important matters of State have been enveloped, the endeavours to keep from the representatives of the people information essential to a right judgment upon passing events, the manner in which the Queen's name has been dragged before the public to crush implacable opponents and screen incompetent friends, all point in one direction, and that direction the most dangerous to English liberty. The respect due to a Sovereign who has served her country long and well makes it difficult to discuss the manner in which the prerogative has been abused. But this respect has been availed of by the Ministry to encroach upon the privileges of Parliament without fear of criticism, and a point seems approaching when, disastrous as it must be to the throne, that respect will be in peril of being swept away by a people loyal to the core, but objecting to the Crown being drawn into the political arena at the bidding of any Ministry for the carrying out of any of its purposes. As long as the Cabinet professes to be constitutional, it must take the responsibility of the Royal actions, not assuming it after, but knowing its weight before the fact, and all advances in favour of making the Crown more powerful than at present must be strenuously resisted. The messages of the Queen and the Duke of Cambridge to Lord Chelmsford, sent on the responsibility of one Minister alone, may have been the mere expressions of goodwill and personal favour into which they have been twisted,* but they form a

* " *From the* SECRETARY OF STATE FOR WAR, *London, to* LORD CHELMSFORD, *Pietermaritzburg* :—The Queen graciously desires me to say she sympathises most sincerely with you in the dreadful loss which has deprived her of so many gallant officers and men, and that *Her Majesty places entire confidence in you* and in the troops to maintain our honour and our good name."—" DUKE OF CAMBRIDGE, *London, to* LORD CHELMSFORD, *Pietermaritzburg* :—

dangerous precedent, and one the present Cabinet may not be trusted to withstand. The effect of Court influence in politics is difficult to estimate and delicate to discuss, but that it has been greater since than before 1876, when on the Royal Titles Bill it first became prominent, is notorious. A word or a hint on a matter of this

Have heard by telegraph of events occurred. Grieved for 24th and others who have fallen victims. Fullest confidence in regiment, and *am satisfied that you have done and will continue to do everything that is right.* Strong reinforcements of all arms ordered to embark at once.—Feb. 13th." The latter despatch was known nothing of in England until, being published by Lord Chelmsford "for the information of those under his command," it returned to this country in the Cape newspapers. It may be remarked in this connection, that the "private communications" of which Sir Robert Peel recently spoke, have never been explained. The right hon. baronet, in the debate on the Zulu War in the House of Commons on March 28th, 1879, said: "The despatch of the 19th of March censures him [Sir Bartle Frere] as strongly as any man was ever censured, though I am told that with that very despatch of censure there went out a private communication urging him in the strongest terms not to resign and not to accept the censure. I want to have a denial of that from the front bench. I believe, and I may say I know, that when the letter of censure went out, on the 19th of March, letters were sent, not only by the Government, but by many persons connected with the Government, begging Sir Bartle Frere not to consider the censure, but to remain at his post and to act as he would wish to act." Colonel Stanley subsequently spoke, but made no reference to this portion of Sir Robert Peel's speech; and in continuation of the debate on March 31st, Viscount Sandon and the Chancellor of the Exchequer spoke, but neither denied Sir Robert Peel's statement.

kind should be sufficient to show the danger and indicate the remedy.

VI.—THE OPPOSITION AND THE DICTATORSHIP.

"It is not Radicalism, it is not the revolutionary spirit of the nineteenth century, which has consigned 'another place' to illustrious insignificance; it is Conservatism and a Conservative Dictator. . . . Something has risen up in this country as fatal in the political world as it has been in the landed world of Ireland —we have a great Parliamentary middleman. It is well-known what a middleman is; he is a man who bamboozles one party and plunders the other, till, having obtained a position to which he is not entitled, he cries out, 'Let us have no party questions, but fixity of tenure.'"—MR. DISRAELI *on Sir Robert Peel*, 1845.

One of the results, and by no means the least inconsiderable, of the policy of the past five years is, that England is more completely at the mercy of one man's caprice than could have been deemed possible under a Constitutional Government. With the present Premier, Ministerial responsibility has become a figment to be thrown aside at will. The principles of "Vivian Grey," and of "Tancred," wild speculations as they appeared when written, have been embodied into English history. In "Vivian Grey" we have a Lord Beaconsfield of fiction, in Mr. Disraeli a Lord Beaconsfield of fact; in "Tancred" we are told that the English want Cyprus, and its author has provided it for us; in "Vivian Grey" politics are declared to have no honour, and the present Government has amply proved it; in "Tancred" the Empress of India is mentioned, and by this Prime Minister she has been created. The dreams of Disraelian youth have become the devices of Beaconsfieldian old age. The nation must pay that the Premier may be proved a prophet.

And when exception is taken to such a course, when it is urged that the State is more to be considered than the statesman, the Constitution than the constitutionalist, the objectors are bidden hold their peace and not disturb the divinity that doth hedge a Prime Minister. An Opposition discharging its recognized and essential duty of criticism is branded as factious, and every effort made to destroy its legitimate influence by opposing to it the wishes of the Crown. Told that they have no right to argue, its members are further informed that their only course is to trust the Ministry and obey its behests. They are asked to trust a Ministry whose members secretly distrust and openly contradict one another;* to trust a Ministry

* The attitude of the Premier during the Eastern crisis towards those of his colleagues who preferred peace will prove this, a most

whose steps have been strewn with broken pledges and abortive projects; to trust a Ministry who, free from the trammels of principle, has revelled in the licence of prerogative. They are bidden have confidence in a Ministry whose Foreign policy has been censured by those who know the most about it; whose Eastern policy has been condemned by Lord Hammond, for many years the Permanent Under-Secretary for Foreign Affairs; whose Zulu policy has been condemned by Sir Henry Holland, formerly permanently connected with the Colonial Office; whose Afghan policy has been condemned by Lords Lawrence and Northbrook, the only two surviving ex-Viceroys. They are asked to follow this Ministry into whatever tortuous paths it may go, asking nothing, hoping nothing, but that somehow, at some time, and

striking example being instanced by Lord Carnarvon in his speech of January 25th, 1878, explaining his resignation: "On the second of this month, as some of your Lordships may remember, I addressed a reply to a deputation which waited upon me in reference to certain questions, in which I spoke of the war and the general attitude of Her Majesty's Government. . . . On the following day, in the Cabinet, the noble Earl *the Prime Minister thought himself at liberty to condemn very severely the language that I had used.* . . . Having vindicated [in a memorandum] the position I had taken, I re-affirmed, in the hearing of my colleagues, and without any contradiction, the propositions that I had then laid down . . . but no public or private disavowal was uttered or hinted at with regard to what I then said."

in some unknown fashion, all may come right. An Opposition that would have consented so to forego its rights and abnegate its functions would deserve the odium sought to be cast upon it. But an Opposition that has refused to be bullied into the acceptance of a dictatorship or cajoled into the extension of the prerogative, has earned its title to the gratitude of the free.

The assumption that it is the custom of an English Opposition to support the existing Government without reserve in times of foreign complication is proved to be gratuitous by the attitude of the present Premier on the Crimean and Chinese wars, and on the Schleswig-Holstein question. As Mr. Disraeli, the leader of the Opposition, he never lost an opportunity, even within a few hours of the outbreak of war, to criticise and condemn the action of those engaged in maintaining the national honour. Taunted in 1854 * with not moving a vote of censure after so much censoriousness, Mr. Disraeli contented himself with the verbal quibble, "I will not propose a vote of no confidence in men who prove to me every hour that they have no confidence in each other." Two months later,† in defending the minutest criticism upon the war estimates,

* March 21st, 1854.   † May 15th, 1854.

he observed: "In my opinion it is better that our foes should see that sums so vast as these . . . should be frankly discussed. . . We will to the utmost do our duty to our constituencies, to see that the ways and means may be adjusted according to the principles of eternal justice." As a fact no one has done more to dispel the theory of party non-interference in foreign politics than the present Premier, and any who know the course of English political history will not need to be told that Oppositions have triumphed and Ministries fallen on questions of war and peace. The assertion so brazenly trumpeted of late, that it is the duty of all good citizens to support the Government at times of crisis, whether that Government is pursuing a worthy or a weak or even a wicked policy, is as untrue to history as to common sense. It may suit the purposes of a patriotism based upon brute force, but not those of a patriotism based upon reason and humanity.

Those who would accuse the Opposition of obstructing business because of their criticisms on foreign affairs forget that no one has oftener than the Premier besought those antagonistic to him to bring matters to a division which, in the present Parliament, was necessarily a foregone conclusion. And if it be added that no objection would be taken if the Opposition formulated an alternative policy, it might not only be replied that on every single one of these foreign differences has the Opposition done so, but that they would not have done so had they followed the precedent laid down by Mr. Disraeli, when he told Lord Palmerston,* "It is not for us, it is not for any man in this House, to indicate to the Ministers what should be the foreign policy of the country. The most we can do, is to tell the noble lord what is not our policy." The Opposition can fairly claim that had their recommendations been followed, the emancipated nations of Eastern Europe would not have been forced to regard England with distrust and Russia with gratitude, Turkey to complain that promises of help had led her into a war she was forced to fight alone, nor Greece to point at us as having held her from victory when it was within her grasp, and then left her to the treacherous procrastination of her ancient foe.

* *Debate on the Schleswig-Holstein Question*, July 4th, 1864.

VII.—THE CHOICE OF POLICIES.

"Let us in this House re-echo that which I believe to be the sovereign sentiment of this country; let us tell persons in high places that cunning is not caution, and that habitual perfidy is not high policy of State .... Let us bring back ... what the country requires, what the country looks for. Let us do it at once in the only way in which it can be done, by dethroning this dynasty of deception, by putting an end to the intolerable yoke of official despotism and Parliamentary imposture."—MR. DISRAELI *on Sir Robert Peel*, March 17th, 1845.

"With no domestic policy, he is obliged to divert the attention of the people from the consideration of their own affairs to the distractions of foreign politics. His external system is turbulent and aggressive, that his rule at home may be tranquil and unassailed. Hence arises excessive expenditure, heavy taxation, and the stoppage of all social improvement. . . . The general policy which I should enforce at this juncture may be contained in these words—'honourable peace, reduced taxation, and social improvement.'"—MR. DISRAELI, *Address to the Electors of Buckinghamshire*, March, 1857.

And now has to be considered that which shortly must occupy the attention of the constituencies—by what policy shall the future be guided? For good or for evil, the next General Election must decide an issue greater than any of the past half-century. Should a Tory Ministry be again returned to power, strong in the condonation of the past, rash in the consciousness of its strength, it may carry the doctrines of Imperialism to a height which nothing but revolution can lower, and sink the fortunes of the country to a depth from which nothing but a miracle can save. If what has been done since 1874 could be the issue of a majority gathered from the four winds of heaven by clamorous sections leagued by self-interest, what might be expected from a majority of like mind, elected on a plain issue, drunk with success, and eager to avenge an attempted check? If the nation does not even yet realize the full force of what its latest exponents mean by Imperialism, a renewed lease of power to the present Ministry would teach the most unteachable that that system is incompatible with progress, antagonistic to liberty, and destructive to the best interests of the people.

But is it a time to be trying Imperialist experiments, to be seeking pretexts for quarrel and opportunities for conquest, when the nation is suffering a distress unparalleled in recent annals? Is it a time to be increasing armaments and looking the wide world through for occasion to fight, when the people are crushed with poverty and longing for peace? Is it a time to extend our dominions when those we already possess demand our every attention? Surely, if there be a time for annexation, there is a time for the cessation of aggrandisement; if there be a time for the havoc of war, there is a time for the blessing of peace; if there be a time for aggressive action, there is a time to rest and be thankful. And if ever a time existed when calm was necessary and strife especially to be abhorred, it is the present,—the present, weary of warfare, wishing for peace.

And this is the issue upon which the country must pronounce—this and this alone is the "burning question" of the hour. For this minor differences must be forgotten, sectional interests unseen. It is no time to argue whether this or that particular question should form the main plank of the Liberal platform. Until the present system be done away with, there can be no Liberal platform but one, and that of a single plank. Upon it Whigs, Moderates, and Radicals can unite without fear and without reserve, and if duty be done as in days that are past there can be no fear for the result. It is time that the nation should speak, and with no faltering voice. The people have asked for the bread of settled policy, decreased taxation, and beneficial reform, and have received the stone of bastard Imperialism, war without glory, and peace without honour. It is for the Liberals once more to prove that the principles which have made this country great can keep her prosperous, that her strength lies not so much in the valour of her armies as in the constancy of her virtues, and that, despite the sneers of those who, admiring despotism abroad, bewail its absence at home, England can hold her influence in Europe, not with the aids of the bully or the arts of the bravo, but with the help of those principles, eternal in their origin and ever developing a nobler growth,—the principles of justice, of honour, and of fair dealing among men.

INDEX.

A

Abortive Projects, 59
Accumulated Expenditure and Increased Taxation, 48
Adderley, Sir Charles, and Merchant Shipping Bill, 75
Administrative Fiascoes, 79
Admiralty's Judgment on *Vanguard* and *Mistletoe* Disasters, 97
Afghan War, the, 34
Agricultural Holdings Bill, 9, 66
Alberta, collision with the, 97
Anderson, Mr., threatens amendment to Rhodope Grant, 83
Andrassy Note, Government's acceptance of, 30
Anglo-Turkish Convention, The, 105
Army Clothing Department, reduction at the, 96
Artizans' Dwellings Act, inutility of, 65
Asia-Minor, English Protectorate of, 105
Atrocities in Bulgaria (*see* Bulgarian Atrocities)

B

Barttelot, Sir W., denounces Government surrender on County Boards, 10
Batoum, Lord Beaconsfield's Description of, 120
Baxter, Mr., moves rejection of Scotch Church Patronage Bill, 59
Beaconsfield, Earl of, on the "consolidation" of Turkey, 31
    ,, On "Peace with honour," 31
    ,, Admits the "very great" distress in the country, 55
    ,, Considers it a "very questionable course to allude publicly to distress," 83
    ,, Recommends "prudence and moderation" to Greece, 103
    ,, On "a scientific frontier," 118
    ,, Description of Batoum contradicted by Hobart Pasha, 120
    ,, Attack on Mr. Gladstone, 121
Beaconsfield, Earl of, denies the existence of dissensions in the Cabinet, 127
    ,, Corrected by Lord Granville, 128
    ,, Directly contradicted by Lord Carnarvon, 131
    ,, Directly contradicted by Lord Northbrook, 132
"Beer and Bible," results of the alliance of, 18
Bentinck, Mr. Cavendish (*Jobs Accomplished*), 94
Berlin Congress, Contradictory opinions on England's Representatives at, 117
Berlin Memorandum, Government's rejection of the, 30
Berlin Treaty, Practical Abrogation of, 30
Birmingham and the Licensing Act, 19
    ,, and the Artizans' Dwellings Act, 66
Bishops in Parliament, 16
Boers, Land Disputes with the Zulus, 43
Booth, Mr. Sclater, on County Boards, 10
    ,, and the "Skeleton" Pollution of Rivers Bill, 61
    ,, Rating Bill, 75
Bosnian Outbreak, the, 26
Bourke, Mr., equivocates on Theodorodi, 133
Bradford, Marquis of Salisbury at, 29
Brewers' Licenses, Remission of, 50
Bright, Mr., and the Royal Titles Bill, 72
Bruce, Mr., Licensing Act, 18
Budgets, Sir Stafford Northcote's Six, 49
Bulgarian Atrocities, Government's indifference to, 30
Bulgaria ruled by a Russian Nominee, 38
Bulwer, Sir Henry, testifies to satisfactory relations to the Zulus and to Cetewayo's good conduct, 42
Burials Question, Government's failure to settle, 15, 62
Burmah (*Wars Threatened*), 26, 32

C

Cabul, the Russian Envoy to, 39
Cambridge and the Licensing Act, 19
Cambridge, Duke of, expresses "fullest confidence" in Lord Chelmsford, 136
Canning, Mr., prefers war to be "rather later than sooner," 29
Canterbury, Archbishop of, on Public Worship Regulation Bill, 13
Carnarvon, Earl of, Resignation of, 128
„ Directly contradicts Lord Beaconsfield, 131
"Caucus," a successful Conservative, 108
Cave, Mr. Stephen, and the Khedive, 95
Cecil, Lord Eustace, and the Army Clothing Department, 96
Central Chamber of Agriculture on Government County Boards Bill, 12
Cetywayo's good conduct testified to by Sir Henry Bulwer, 43
Chambers of Agriculture and the Government County Boards Bill, 11
„ and proposed Clerical Exemption from Rates, 17
Chamberlain, Sir Neville, mission to Cabul, 39
Chatham, its action at last General Election, 22
Chefket Pasha (*Duties Evaded*), 102
Chelmsford, Lord, Royal Message to, 118, 135
„ Duke of Cambridge's message to, 135
Choice of Policies, the, 143
Church and Conservative Alliance, 12
Civil Servants, the (*Harassed Interests*), 21
Clerical Exemption from Rates proposed, 16
Clerks in the dockyards, grievances of, 23
Cockburn, Lord Chief Justice, request for Galley's pardon refused, 98
Colonial Marriages Bill, the Government and the, 16, 111
Colorado beetle, Government's inability to capture, 63
Commons Act, 77
Constantinople Conference, failure of the, 30
Contagious Diseases (Animals) Act, 12, 74
County Boards, Mr. Read's motion, 10
„ Government opposition and ultimate acceptance, 11
Cranbrook, Viscount, requests Lord Lytton to make himself certain of his facts, 39
Cranbrook, Viscount, Declines to take Lord Lytton's advice immediately to declare war, 41
„ Ability to mislead, 123
Cross, Mr., Licensing Bill, 18
„ On the "illogical idea of the publicans," 19
„ And the "Local Option" principle, 20
„ Fails to carry Scotch Under-Secretary Bill, 64
„ Factory Bill, 75
„ And the Labour Laws, 76
„ "Plank Bed," Prisons Act. 78
„ Believes there has been " a lying spirit abroad," 125
„ Equivocates on Theodorodi, 133
Cyprus, acquisition of, 105

D

"Dear Meat" Bill, 12, 74
Deficit and Distress, 54
Demand for Dissolution, 1
Derby, Earl of, on the possibility of war, 28
„ Compared by Lord Salisbury to "Titus Oates," 131
Devonport, its action at last General Election, 23
Dillwyn, Mr. and the Slade Appointment, 87
Disestablishment Movement in Scotland strengthened by the Government, 15
„ Mr. Gladstone's opinion of, 60
Disraeli, Mr., on "Plundering and Blundering," 3
„ Describes Conservative Theory and Practice, 5
„ Opposes the Malt Tax, 8
„ Ridicules "a religious cry," 12
„ Wishes to "put down Ritualism," 13
„ Believes in beer as "a necessary of life," 17
„ Ridicules "a very spirited policy," 25
„ As Chancellor of the Exchequer, 25
„ Denounces "a dictatorial policy," 26
„ Would "settle the Eastern Question in a month" if he were disposed, 26
„ Disapproves a "turbulent and aggressive" policy, 27

INDEX. 149

Disraeli, Mr., considers the Crimean War unnecessary, 27
  ,, Supports the Principle of Non-intervention, 27
  ,, Objects to "turbulent diplomacy," 28
  ,, Opposes Lord Palmerston's "most rash and imprudent system," 29
  ,, Thinks even "necessary and just" war may be prevented by "astute and skilful management," 34
  ,, On "The Higher Principles of Humanity," and "The National Interests," 34
  ,, Testifies to the "laudable promptitude" of Mr. Gladstone's Government, 47
  ,, Condemns "a war expenditure in time of peace," 49
  ,, Against "any extravagantly-conceived military establishments," 54
  ,, Describes Conservatism as "an unhappy cross-breed," 58
  ,, Throws blame on draughtsmen for Reactionary clauses of Endowed Schools Bill, 69
  ,, Refuses to make any concession on Education Bill, 71
  ,, Introduces the "Empress Bill," 72
  ,, Mythical reference to the wishes of the Native Princes, 72
  ,, Withdraws the Merchant Shipping Bill of 1875, 75
  ,, In the "Realms of Fancy," 81
  ,, On the Fitzgerald Appointment, 90
  ,, Charges the Press with corruption, 99
  ,, Thinks Mr. Gladstone "unnecessarily alarmed," 101
  ,, Holds that "in politics there is no honour," 113
  ,, Promises to repeal the Income Tax, 114
  ,, Describes the Bulgarian Atrocities as "coffee-house babble," 116
  ,, Characterises Lord Salisbury as "a great master of gibes and flouts and jeers," 125
  ,, Excuse that "a good deal has happened," 116

Disraeli, Mr., in favour of "honourable peace, reduced taxation, and social improvement," 143
Distress, Lord Beaconsfield's opinion on the, 55
Dockyardsmen, grievances of the, 22
Dog Tax, Increase of, 52
Duchy of Lancaster Contracts out of Agricultural Holdings Act, 10
Duties Evaded, 101

E.

Eastern Question, The Government and the, 26
Eastern Roumelia ruled by a Russian Nominee, 31
Education Act Amendment Bill. 15
Egypt (*Wars Threatened*), 26, 32
Elphinstone, Sir James (*Jobs Accomplished*), 93
Endowed Schools Bill, 15, 67
Engine Room Artificers, Grievance of the, 23
Episcopate, Increase of the, 16

F.

Factory Bill, 75
Failures, Fiascoes, and Fables, 57
Farmers, The (*Harassed Interests*), 6
Fawcett, Mr., Vital Amendment on Endowed Schools Bill, 68
Finance, Tory and Liberal, 54
Fitzgerald, Sir Seymour (*Jobs Accomplished*).
Forster, Mr., moves rejection of Endowed Schools Bill, 67, 69
Frere, Sir Bartle, recommending that "something should be done" in Afghanistan, 42
  ,, Ultimatum to Cetewayo, 44
Friendly Societies Act, 66, 76

G.

Galley, Government refusal to pardon, 98
Gladstone, Mr., on Sir Stafford Northcote's Sinking Fund, 50
  ,, On the Disestablishment movement in Scotland, 60
  ,, On Government Savings Banks Bill, 61
  ,, Denounces Endowed Schools Bill, 68
  , On Sir D. Lange's dismissal, 101
Granville, Earl, corrects Lord Beaconsfield, 128

I I

Greece, the Government's promise to aid, 30
Greek Claims, England and (*Duties Evaded*), 102
Greenwich, its Action at last General Election, 22
,, Grievances of the Pensioners, 24
Gundamak, Treaty of, 47

H.

Hampton, Lord (*Jobs Accomplished*), 88
Harassed Interests, 5
Hardy, Mr. Gathorne, and the Regimental Exchanges Bill, 70
Harrowby, Earl of, Defeats Government Burials Bill, 63
Hartington, Marquis of, moves Resolution Disapproving Government's Education Bill, 71
Hicks-Beach, Sir Michael, and Sir Bartle Frere, 46
,, Asserts that the Distress had been much exaggerated for Party purposes, 82
,, Opposes Irish Sunday Closing Bill, 110
,, Supports Irish Sunday Closing Bill, 111
,, Moves Resolution against "Empress" title, 73
Hobart Pasha contradicts Lord Beaconsfield's Description of Batoum, 120
Holms, Mr. John, disproves a Disraelian assertion, 81
Hull and the Licensing Act, 19
Hypothec, Government attitude towards, 113

I.

Imperialism, 133
Income Tax, Fluctuations of the, 49
Income Tax, Mr. Disraeli's Promise to Repeal, 114
India, Proposed Loan of Ten Millions to, 86
India Vernacular Press Act, 100
Irish Intermediate Education Act, 78
Irish University Education, 85
Irish Sunday Closing, 19, 110

J.

Jobs Accomplished, 86
Judicature Bill, 60, 108

L.

Labour Laws, Amendment of, 76
Layard, Mr., the appointment of, 30

Lange, Sir Daniel (*Duties Evaded*), 101
Legislative Failures, 58
Leiningen, The Government and Prince, 97
Lewis, Mr. C. E., and the Parliamentary Privileges of the Press, 109
Licensing Act Amendment Bill, 18
Lytton, Lord, appointed Viceroy of India, 35
,, Informs Lord Salisbury he has found the "opportunity and pretext hitherto wanting" in Afghanistan, 36
,, Forwards Alarmist Telegrams respecting Russian Envoy, 38
,, Urges Immediate Declaration of War, 40

M.

Malt Tax, Proposed Repeal of, 8
Marvin Memorandum, The, 30, 130
Merchant Shipping Bill, The, 75
Ministerial Fables, 113
Mistletoe Disaster, The, 97
Montagu, Lord Robert, proposes that the "twenty-fifth" clause be made compulsory, 72
Mundella, Mr., and Endowed Schools Bill, 69
,, Factory Bill adopted by Government, 75
Municipal Qualifications Abolition Bill, 113

N.

Nonconformists, the Government and the, 15
Non-intervention, the Ministry and, 27
Northbrook, Lord, Directed to "find, or, if need be, to create," a pretext to quarrel with Shere Ali, 35
,, Directly contradicts Lord Beaconsfield, 132
Northcote, Sir Stafford, on the Malt Tax, 8
,, And Agricultural Holdings Act, 10
,, As Chancellor of the Exchequer, 25
,, Denies that the Afghan policy had been changed, 38
,, Six Budgets, 49
,, Savings Banks Bill, 61
,, Repudiates Lord Sandon on Endowed Schools Bill, 86

INDEX. 151

Northcote, Sir Stafford, Repudiates Lord Sandon on Education Bill, 72
" Friendly Societies Act, 66, 76
" Proposes Rhodope Grant, 83
" Withdraws Rhodope Grant, 84
" on the Slade appointment, 87
" Explains away Mr. Ward Hunt's "Paper Fleet," 108
" Repudiates Mr. Stanhope on Stock Exchange Commission, 112
" Repudiates Mr. Lowther on Irish Land Act Committee, 113
" Thinks it would be "wrong and culpable to repeal the Income Tax," 115
" Describes a statement of Lord Beaconsfield's as "a figure of speech," 119
" Says the Government "has no concealed designs," 129

O.

Ogle, Mr. (*Duties Evaded*), 102
Opposition and the Dictatorship, 137
Oxford and the Licensing Act, 19

P.

Patronage in Scotland, The Government and, 15
"Peace with Honour," 31
Peel, Sir Robert, alleges "Private Communications" had been sent to Sir Bartle Frere, 136
Pell, Mr., introduces Amendment Dissolving School Boards, 71
Pelly, Sir Lewis, and the Peshawur Conference, 37
Permissive Bills, The Government's, 65
Personal Government and Imperialism, 133
Peshawur Conference, The, 37
Piggott, Mr. (*Jobs Accomplished*), 90
Plimsoll, Mr., coerces Government into passing their Merchant Shipping Bill, 75
Poor Law Amendment Act Amendment Bill, 113

Portsmouth, Its Action at last General Election, 22
Priests, The (*Harassed Interests*), 12
Prisons Act, 78
Private Yards *versus* Public Yards, 23
Proposals Withdrawn, 79
Promise and the Performance, 3
Publicans, The (*Harassed Interests*), 17
Public Houses, Hours of Closing, 18
Public Worship Regulation Bill, 13

R.

Rating Bill, 75
Reactionary Measures, 67
Read, Mr. C. S., on Failure of Agricultural Holdings Act, 10
" County Boards Motion, 10
" Threatens to Obstruct Government Valuation Bill, 11
" Denounces Government County Boards Bill, 12
Regimental Exchanges Bill, 70
Reserves, Government Treatment of the, 96
Rhodope Grant, The, 82
Richmond, Duke of, Agricultural Holdings Bill, 9
" Contracts out of Agricultural Holdings Act, 67
" Declares Marvin Memorandum to be inaccurate, 130
" Fails to carry "Sanitary" Burials Bill, 62
Ritualism, Mr. Disraeli's Attempt to "Put Down," 13
Rothschild, Messrs., receive Commission on Suez Canal Shares, 105
Royal Message to Lord Chelmsford, 118, 135
Royal Titles Bill, 72
Russia (*Wars Threatened*), 26

S.

Salisbury, Marquis of, on Mr. Disraeli, the Political "Weathercock," 5
" Upholds Non-Intervention, 29
" Refuses to "Sustain the Turkish Empire by Force of Arms," 29
" Despatch on "All Fools' Day," 30
" Promises the "Literal Fulfilment of the Berlin Treaty," 31

Salisbury, Marquis of, directs Lord Northcote to "find, or, if need be, to create" a pretext to quarrel with Shere Ali, 35
„ Denies any Interference with the Ameer, 38, 126
„ Denounces the Disraelian "Policy of Legerdemain," 57
„ Fails to carry Pollution of Rivers Bill, 62
„ Objects to "Tampering with the Purity of Truth," 119
„ Describes a statement of Mr. Disraeli's as "a Simple and Absolute Fabrication," 126
„ On "Our Old Friends the Newspapers," 127
„ Declares the Marvin Memorandum as "not Deserving of Confidence," 130
„ Compares Lord Derby to "Titus Oates," 131
„ Denies that Government has censured Sir Bartle Frere, 133
Samuelson, Mr. B., on Failure of Agricultural Holdings Act, 9
„ and Royal Titles Bill, 73
Sandon, Viscount, and Agricultural Holdings Act, 10
„ on the Endowed Schools Bill and the Nonconformists, 15, 67
„ Education Bill of 1876, 15, 71
Savings Banks Bill, 61
"Scientific Frontier," 118
Scotch Church Patronage Bill, 15, 59
Scotch Under-Secretary Bill, 64
Selwin-Ibbetson, Sir H., and the Grievances of the Civil Servants, 22
Sheep Dogs Taxed by the Conservatives, 7
Shere Ali and Lord Lytton, 36
Simon, Serjeant, on Conditions of Granting New Licenses, 20
Sinking Fund, Establishment of, 50
Slade, Sir Alfred (*Jobs Accomplished*), 87
Slave Circulars, The, 79
Smith, Mr. W. H., and the Grievances of the Civil Servants, 22
Stanhope, Mr. E., and the Indian Ten Millions Loan, 86

Stanley, Col., and the Grievances of the Civil Servants, 22
„ On the Wellesley Appointment, 92
Stansfeld, Mr., Rating Bill adopted by Government, 75
"*Startling*" *Successes*, 74
Suez Canal Shares, Purchase of the, 105
Sugar Duties, Abolition of, 49
Sunday Closing in England, 19
„ „ in Ireland, 19, 110
Supplementary Estimates, Government's Abuse of, 51

T.

Taxation, The Increase of, 48
Theodorodi, Release of, 98, 133
Threatened Wars, 26
Tobacco Duty, Increase of, 52
Tory and Liberal Finance, 54
Tory Policy and the Public Purse, 25
Transvaal, Annexation of, 43
Treasury Bench Vacillation, 107
Treaty of Paris, Abrogation of, 31
Turkey Refuses to Keep Faith with Greece, 30

U.

Uncalled-for Undertaken, 105

V.

Vanguard Disaster, The, 97
Vivisection Act, 77
Vote of Credit, 52

W.

Ward Hunt, Mr., on Sheep Dog Tax, 7
„ „ as Chancellor of the Exchequer, 25
„ „ on "A Paper Fleet," 107
Wars Threatened, 26
Wars Commenced, 34
Wellesley, Colonel (*Jobs Accomplished*), 91
Whitbread, Mr., proposes to Cancel the Slave Circulars, 81
Wild Fowl Preservation Act, 77
Winter Assize Act, 77

Y.

Yakoob Khan, 35

Z.

Zulu War, The, 34
Zulu Land Disputes with the Boers, 43

www.ingramcontent.com/pod-product-compliance
Lightning Source LLC
Chambersburg PA
CBHW030256170426
43202CB00009B/758